RIDE ON

ADVENTURES IN TRAUMATIC BRAIN INJURY

Greg Nordfelt
With Sheila Ashdown

Calliope
Press

Cover designed by Michael Sheen

Greg Nordfelt
www.gregnordfelt.com

Printed in the United States of America

First Printing: October 2018
Calliope Press

ISBN- 978-0-578-40335-9

Dedicated to Laura, my best friend, my lover, my wife.

It's "You & Me"

PRAISE FOR RIDE ON

"Greg's story is a compelling tale on how someone strives to create a new life after a Traumatic Brain Injury. It is required reading for anyone who has experienced a TBI or anyone who lives with a TBI survivor."

—*Dr. Andrew Dodds*, MD, MPH, *Physical & Rehabilitation Electrodiagnostic Medicine, Intermountain Medical Center*

"A masterful, triumphant tome that captivates the senses and stirs the soul...Hop onto a Harley and take a perilous journey through the world of TBI injury and recovery. Nordfelt's account is both riveting and educational, directly challenging Sisyphean attitudes with his own perseverance. In "Ride On," Nordfelt proves that the mind is resilient, spirits can be restored, and the soul is divined for rebirth."

—*Dana M. Lewis*, *Former Personal Aide to President and First Lady Obama*

"Greg and Laura Nordfelt have demonstrated a powerfully potent blend of determination and optimism in their mutual recovery from Greg's traumatic brain injury several years ago. Their story provides hope to anyone working to overcome a seemingly insurmountable challenge."

—*Harris H. Simmons*, *Chairman and CEO, Zions Bancorporation*

"As a TBI survivor, I know firsthand how a traumatic brain injury can dramatically change not only your life, but how you see, think, feel—who you are. Greg Nordfelt offers wisdom and humor, authenticity and a practical guide for living a powerful life after TBI. Ride On is a powerful, brave, and hilarious adventure...a must read if you've been touched by traumatic brain injury."

—*Angie Fenimore*, *International Bestselling Author, author trainer at Calliope Writing Coach, co-host of the award-winning Calliope Writing Coach Podcast*

"Greg's story is one of teamwork, love, skill, and perseverance. In healthcare, we are privileged to care for our neighbors when they are facing life's greatest challenges. I'm glad that Intermountain Healthcare was "there" for Greg when he needed us."

—*A. Marc Harrison*, MD, *President and CEO Intermountain Healthcare*

3

"Mr. Greg Nordfelt is a prime example of the importance of developing an interdisciplinary system of care for the treatment of trauma patients, especially patients with severe traumatic brain injury. The care of these patients is a group effort of caring physicians, nurses, therapists and involves most departments of a hospital working collaboratively to produce superior outcomes. Deliberate attention to details and consistency of care in the treatment of traumatic brain injury patients is the difference between a functional recovery versus a permanent disability."

—Dr. William Ganz, MD, Neurosurgeon Kootenai Health, Former Chief of Neurosurgery St. Paul Medical Center, Asst Professor of Neurosurgery University of Minnesota

"A deeply personal look into the experience of traumatic brain injury. Greg Nordfelt's story and his incredible recovery will be a lifeline for the loved ones of any person struggling through the long road to recovery after a traumatic brain injury. Anyone who has suffered TBI will able to identify with the challenges Greg faced as he clawed his way back into life. The amazing part of this story is the changes he experiences and his ability to relate to others. There is hope!"

—Dr. Joseph Bowen, MD, Orthopedic Surgeon, Kootenai Health

"Every health care encounter, no matter how simple or how complex, is an act of compassion. There is a joy that comes from bringing our technical expertise to the aid of those who need it, but it is a special honor, to share in the celebration of a life restored. Thank you, Greg, for allowing Kootenai Health to be part of your celebration."

—Jon Ness, CEO, Kootenai Health

FOREWORD

When my friend Greg Nordfelt crashed his motorcycle, and was immediately faced with a long, grueling rehabilitation that required him to relearn how to talk, read, write and walk, he had a marvelous experience that most of us will never have. In fact, it was one of those envious experiences that forever changes our lives and makes us either bitter or better. Psychologists call these experiences "Significant Emotional Events."

A Significant Emotional Event or S.E.E. is an experience we use as a mile-marker on our road of life that allows us to pause and measure what we believed and how we behaved before the S.E.E. occurred, and how we now think and behave differently because it occurred. The operative words being believe, before and because.

I say this particular S.E.E. is an envious experience because it forced Greg to challenge a default phrase we all have over-used, and to come to grips with true reality. You see, when most of us make a horrible decision that leaves us disappointed, discouraged, decimated and alone, or are blindsided by an angry divorce, the loss of a loved one, or the loss of a job, we usually explain our devastation with the familiar, "I hit rock bottom."

However, when Greg crashed and found himself in a hospital bed with a serious Traumatic Brain Injury the only way he was ever going to recover was to realize that no, he did not hit rock bottom. He hit rock foundation. He hit his rock beliefs. He hit his baseline core values and his bottom-line governing principles. He was once again introduced to the significant importance of love, deep human connection, gratitude, service before self, and the realization that what matters most is what lasts the longest.

Greg's story isn't one of loss and pain, but rather, a symbol of incredible gain with a new-found opportunity to prove that self is not discovered. Self is created. No matter what our past has been, we have a spotless future. Greg confesses that his recovery was not a miracle. It occurred because of his previously learned rock-solid foundational understanding of the universal law of the harvest—we reap only that which we sow. As business philosopher Jim Rohn so eloquently said, "Life responds to deserve and not to need. It doesn't say, 'If you need, you will reap.' It says, 'If you plant, you will reap.'" In other words, specific results are achieved because of specific beliefs that are linked to specific hardcore tasks, most of which are learned through experience, acknowledging that nothing happens to us—it always happens for us.

In his eloquent first-person prose, you will quickly realize that Greg's writing style and life-changing wisdom actually uncover powerful nuggets that teach correct principles and inspire us to govern ourselves. As you dive into this remarkable read, Greg invites you to hop on the back of his Harley Davidson with the wind in your face cruising on a winding road through the beautiful landscape of northern Idaho, a ride that leaves you unconscious and fighting for life.

Good News / Bad News

The bad news is that Greg had to go through this catastrophic ordeal in order to learn the lessons he needed to break through his limiting beliefs, redefine what was possible and recommit to becoming everything he was born to be. The good news is that in the pages of this amazing book, Greg has quantified the principled centered truths that he learned and has chronicled his many thrills of victory and agonies of defeat to illuminate a course that we too, can choose to follow without experiencing a life-threatening accident. Voila! His clever and compelling title: Ride On: Adventures in Traumatic Brain Injury.

Clearly, Greg learned through his accident, injury and long arduous rehabilitation, that formal education will make you a living, but it is self-education that will make you a fortune. And clearly, it was this school of hard knocks (in his case, 'College of Crash Dummies') that he acquired outside of his University of Utah MBA training that qualified him to teach the world why and how he was able to go back to work; why and how he was able to keep his marriage intact, and how he has become a best-selling author, an incredible motivational speaker, and a high-performance business coach.

It's been said that the illiterate of the 21st century will not be those who cannot read and write, but those who cannot learn, unlearn, and relearn. This makes Greg's accident one of the most important things that have ever happened to him. No, it wasn't the crash that was important. It was what he learned from it, and who he became as a man, and what he was taught about passionate purpose, the sanctity of life and prioritizing time as a result of going through this setback, that makes it one of the most important and Significant Emotional Events in his life.

When Greg started out to write this memoir he began with a focused expectation that it would be a wonderful motivational/inspirational tale that documented his motorcycle accident and recovery that would teach the world about Traumatic Brain Injuries and how he recovered. However, what Greg produced is a compelling motivational menu of mental meals that presents amazing life lessons that will not only minister to those with TBI and the parents, friends and loved ones who are their care-givers, but this book will nourish the needs and strengthen the souls of every one of us who desires to redefine what's possible and become healthier, happier human beings.

If you are one who has lived a cautious, risk-free life in a safe place void of danger and glamorous adventure, this book is a must read. Because I have read it and re-read it, I will never again fear getting knocked down or use the lame explanation that I hit rock bottom when things didn't go as planned. For Greg has taught the world that today we've never been this old before, and today we'll never be this young again—so right now, and every right now matters. Which means by the time you have digested the morsels of wisdom served to you on the pages of this memoir, I am confident you will forever 'Ride On' and rise each time you fall because of an up-leveled, upgraded foundational belief that you now call your own. In my own words I offer a summarization of the ten truths I've learned from studying this incredible book:

1) Attitude really is everything. Only when your attitude is right, can your abilities catch up.

2) Adversity is what introduces you to yourself and makes you either bitter or better. Which means you can never know what you're made of until you're tested.

3) Pain is a signal to grow, not to suffer. Once we learn the lesson the pain is teaching us the pain goes away. In life there are no mistakes, only lessons.

4) You shouldn't be so quick to claim your limitations when perhaps you've never truly tested them. You never know how strong you are until being strong is the only choice you have.

5) The greatest mistake you can make in life is to continually fear you will make one.

6) The start is what stops most people.

7) When you take a chance on doing just once what others say you can't do, you will never pay attention to their limitations again.

8) Endurance is not just the ability to bear a hard thing, but to turn it into glory.

9) It takes courage to grow up and become who you really are.

10) Which together mean: We can't always control what happens, but we can always control what happens next—especially when we refuse to let what we cannot do interfere with what we can do.

I highly recommend that you buy multiple copies to give to your family members, coworkers and significant friends. Thank you, Greg, for writing this magnificent and monumental masterpiece that adds to your already existing legacy of laughter, learning, leadership and love.

—**Dan Clark**, *NYT Bestselling Author, Hall of Fame Speaker, International Radio Host*

PROLOGUE

D id you know you can have "good coma" days and "bad coma" days? You can—and I'd just had a bad one. It was Thursday, August 18, 2011, and I'd been in a coma for four days. The previous day had been a "bad coma" day. My neurosurgeon, Dr. William Ganz, had slapped his hands together in front of my face, yelled out my name, and tapped on my sternum—all in hopes of getting a response. But nothing. I was non-responsive.

But this was a new day. I lay propped up in bed in an intensive care unit, with my wife, Laura, at my side.

Suddenly, I opened my eyes.

I started scanning the room, trying to take in and make sense of my surroundings. I noticed my leg sticking out in front of me, wrapped in a bulbous bandage. I was covered in wires and tubes and surrounded by machines. I looked straight ahead at the wall. Then I panned to the left, where I saw a nurse standing at the corner of my bed. She was a stranger to me, and I found myself trying to grasp who she was. And then I tried to figure out *where* I was. Everything was odd to me, and I couldn't make sense of it.

And then, I blurted out my first words:

"What ... the?"

To my right, Laura immediately busted up laughing. It was a humorous moment that she needed dearly in the midst of a very intense situation. Even the nurse joined in. (My sister Debbie, who only ever sees the best in me, later insisted that my foul language was the result of my head injury.)

"He's baaaack," Laura said, laughing and relieved.

Of course, I wasn't really back. Not completely. The nurse conducted a physical assessment, which I passed—I could squeeze her hand and wiggle my toes. But from a neurological perspective, I was whacked.

9

"What's your name?" the nurse asked.

"Beauford."

"Where are you from?"

"North Carolina."

"What's your wife's name?"

"Suzy."

Hmm. Considering that my name is Greg, I live in Salt Lake City, Utah, and my wife's name is Laura, it appeared I had a long way to go. I was in between zones, not really *here* and not really *there*. One moment I was in reality; the next moment, I was back in my happy place. But Laura had seen me scanning my environment, gathering bits of information; this first moment was the start of a journey in healing, and also, though I didn't know it at the time, my journey toward discovering a new self. The old Greg was gone.

1

I'll never forget the first time I walked into the Harley-Davidson shop in Salt Lake. The room was packed with bikes, parked inches from each other, and the walls were covered floor to ceiling with leather and Harley-branded *everything*— vests, boots, jackets, chaps, helmets, socks, bikinis, jewelry, gloves, patches, do-rags. Everything. And then there was the gleam from the endless chrome that hung on the walls and windows for your viewing pleasure. Chrome that called out to you; you swore it knew you personally, because Harley makes chrome parts specifically designed for all their bikes—especially for the model you were eyeballing to take home that day.

The atmosphere of the Harley store was filled with the scents of leather, rubber, fresh oil, and hardened steel, all mixed with that "new car" smell. You know, that smell you pay forty grand for at the car dealership and you hope doesn't go away when you drive it off the lot, even though you know your kids will eventually spill Happy Meals all over the brand-new leather seats? That smell that will soon be replaced when you take the team to a rainy soccer match and your car is filled with muddy cleats, grass-stained shin guards, and sweaty uniforms. Or the cheer squad, who wants to ride in your car because you're the "fun" parents, and you've got a bunch of girls who don't like to wear their shoes after a game and their bare feet are on your brand-new floor mats.

Well, that's just not going to happen in a shop full of "Hogs." Here, it's that new Harley smell, *squared.*

As you can maybe tell, this was my first time buying a Harley-Davidson. It was 2001, and I'd just graduated from an executive MBA program. To say it had been a rough couple of years would be a massive understatement. I'd gone through the twenty-two-month program while maintaining a full-time career in commercial lending.

My wife, Laura, and I have a blended family of six kids, all of whom had their own activities, and there were many sports games and performances I had to miss—and that killed me, because I was normally the kind of dad who showed up for absolutely everything. Our daughter Tristen was a gymnast, and she and our daughter Jodi were big into cheerleading; our son Jeremy is the artist of the family and always had a theater or singing performance in production; Ryan and Josh were both accomplished athletes and had games all over the region multiple times a week. Our daughter Jaci was living with her dad several counties away, and so we made time to visit her. For me, since I only had my kids every other weekend, it was crucial to attend as many of those events as possible so I could have a good connection with them. Family has always been a huge priority for me, and with the challenges of blending a family, my time together with them was really important.

The strain was also taking a toll on me physically. I'm normally an active guy, and all of my self-care stuff—skiing, softball, cycling, basketball—went right out the window. In its place was stress-eating. When I get stressed, I *binge*. Hostess Zingers were a fave...cheese fries...double-shot mochas with whip to make it through class and study group... And the result was evident in the thirty-plus pounds I put on in just two years.

But I'm a committed man. When I take on something, I end up doing it no matter the physical stressors it puts on my body. I was proud of my 3.9 grade point average and completing my course with honors, but, boy, did I pay for it.

My parents were proud too, and they sat with Laura and our children in the Huntsman Center for my MBA graduation ceremonies at the University of Utah. I was the youngest of six, and I was a "mistake." Well, that's putting it lightly. There are six years between me and my closest sister, Debbie, and our family didn't have much money. When my dad found out my mom was pregnant with me, he drove to Idaho and got a vasectomy because that procedure wasn't really deemed "acceptable" in Salt Lake in the '60s. Being a "mistake" has been the family joke throughout my life. Though, to be honest, my parents never brought it up, because they loved me at an unbelievable level. I've always thought it was funny as hell that my dad drove to Idaho to get snipped. It still makes me laugh.

When my name was called to get my diploma, my dad sobbed on Laura's shoulder. I was the first of my siblings to receive a graduate degree and only the second, besides my sister Susan, to graduate from college. My dad didn't receive his college degree until he took early retirement in the '80s after being a bookkeeper for three decades. World War Two and the Great Depression kept him from going to college after high school in Salina, Utah. Laura told me my mom and dad "busted their buttons" watching me get my MBA. I could thank them for instilling in me a good work ethic.

When I was growing up, my dad and mom almost always had more than one job. On top of working as a bookkeeper, my dad drove a cab and worked as a janitor, among other odd jobs. My mom did soldering for an electronics company, and she'd frequently come home with burns on her hands. I'd go with both of them to do janitorial work at an office building in downtown Salt Lake. Through them, I learned to work.

To celebrate my academic accomplishment, I was jonesing for a Harley-Davidson. I'd never owned a motorcycle, but I'd ridden them off and on throughout my life. During my childhood, we lived near farmland on the outskirts of the suburbs, and I grew up with about a dozen boys my age. There was usually somebody among us who had a dirt bike, and we loved to make trails and jumps. I'd ridden my friends' enduros, too, but I'd never ridden a Harley. They're a different beast. They're cruisers, meant for slower, more leisurely rides than a bullet bike. I was just looking to experience the wind in my hair and have fun.

Fortunately, Laura was totally on board with the idea of the Harley. She's always been active, and adventure has been a keystone of our marriage, starting with our honeymoon cruise in the western Caribbean. Our first stop was Cozumel, the island off the coast of Mexico. We got off the ship, took the ferry ride to a Mexican town whose name we couldn't pronounce, Playa del Carmen, and spent the day on an amazing beach with powdered-sugar sand and clear, turquoise blue water that we snorkeled in and could see over a hundred feet deep. It was paradise. Everyone was laid-back, warm, and nonjudgmental; they didn't care who we were, what we wore—or didn't wear—or what we ate or drank. No one was watching over us and telling us what to do, like we were used to in our culture back home. It was a taste of something we were missing in our lives. We lived in a very conservative part of the country. So, when Laura and I were "out of the zip code," so to speak, we could be who we really were. We tried new things. Experimented. It was a taste of freedom and authentic living that we hadn't experienced before.

Before we got married in 1994, we went to a marriage counselor, because we knew blending a family would be a challenge. The counselor gave us the best marriage advice we ever received. She said, "In order for you to successfully blend your family, you need to make time for yourselves at least once a month, away from home. It can be a Motel 6. It doesn't matter. As long as it's away from your children for a night." We learned quickly that we had to take care of our marriage to be good blended-family parents. We loved our children so much that we had to love each other first.

We took her advice seriously and have done everything possible, within reason, to find time for our marriage every month. We used to have a boat that we kept at Lake Powell in southern Utah, and even when I was in my MBA program, we'd go to Lake Powell for the weekend and I'd bring my homework to do on the boat.

I'm a banker, so, as you can imagine, I'm very cost conscious. When I was at the Harley shop, face-to-face with those prices, I was thinking to myself, "Holy crap, these are expensive as hell!" I was having sticker shock right out of the chute. I couldn't believe I was actually doing this. We were already in over our heads. We had six kids to support, not to mention the house, cars, a boat, toys—you name it.

But...I was doing well in my career, Laura owned her own business, and was planning to get her emergency medical technician (EMT) certification. My employer had just paid for me to get a master's degree, and I'd just finished an intense two years. I deserved a treat—at least, that's what I was telling myself. And Laura told me as I was getting close to completing my Executive MBA program, "Honey, let's get you a BIG graduation present."

The least expensive Harley is a sportster, and the least expensive sportster is an 883. But...I couldn't get an 883. I would lose respect. It would look bad. If I was going to get a sportster, it would have to be the 1200. That way I could at least hold my head high with some amount of biker street cred.

Plus, in my mind, it couldn't be just any Harley. It had to have an "old school" raised nameplate. Some Harleys have painted logos on the gas tank. Oh no! A painted logo wouldn't do. I had to squeeze my fat, post-grad butt between all the bikes until I found the Sportster that had the best Harley-Davidson emblem. And I found it. It was a classic nameplate, seven inches long, raised, in crimson red, with the name written out horizontally like on the original bikes in 1903. "Harley" on top and "Davidson," slightly off-centered and to the right, underneath. And the emblem was on a "Harley White" gas tank, with mid-rise rolled "Easy Rider" chopper handle bars. It was calling out to me. Damn, how could I say no to that white H-D goddess with red sparkling eyes.

The next step was to glance around and see if anyone was looking. I've sat on a ton of dirt bikes in my life. This wasn't my first rodeo, for crying out loud. But it was my first time sitting on a Harley. And these motorcycles aren't small. Sportsters are the smallest of the Harleys, but they're still bigger than the bikes I was used to riding. A lot bigger. But the benefit is that they're closer to the ground, which was better for me because my legs are, well, short. I have a thirty-inch inseam. (Okay, you got me—It's really twenty-nine.)

I looked around again. When I thought the coast was clear, I put my left hand on the rubber-and-chrome grip. It felt like I had just laid hands on the Holy Grail in a Monty Python movie. I started to raise my right leg when I heard the dreaded, "Dude, can I help you?"

I found out that day that long-bearded Harley salespeople might look rough, but they're freakin' awesome! He let me sit on as many Sportsters as I wanted, because, you know what? That's how you fall in love and buy one. Once I felt the bike between my legs and saw the chrome dial eyeballing me, it was just a matter of time before I leaned forward and grabbed the throttle with my right hand, put my left hand on the grip, centered the bike, and raised the kickstand. Then I began to get a sense of the majesty of what I knew was the world's most revered motorcycle. I was sitting on a grand machine manufactured by an American company that was just two years shy of breaking the hundred-year mark. And already I knew this Harley was energy, space, time, and the speed of light. It had to be *mine*.

My new Harley friend explained leather vests and how they identify bikers and separate us from the rest of the world. He demonstrated how leather chaps are worn and how they protect motorcyclists from dreaded "road rash" and burns from the engine and exhaust. I was thinking to myself, *I thought chaps were a cowboy thing.*

He showed me what to look for in a helmet and said, "Since your forehead is freakin' huge, you have to fit and strap it tight to make sure it doesn't slide back and rest on top of your head—that would be a waste of a good helmet." Hmmm. Then he showed me leather jackets that had protection. More money. Thoughts for another day.

Then he asked if I wanted to upgrade with more chrome, and I mumbled something like, "Yeaaah." Then he said, "Would you like it to be faster?" I said, "Okay," slightly drooling. Then he asked the magic question: "Should we make your Sportster louder with straighter chromed pipes that integrate into the upgraded airflow system?" And I screamed, "Hells yeah!"

So, I did it. The down payment was made, the papers were drawn. Done.

Funny thing was, I didn't even have a motorcycle license. So the Harley shop took care of getting my new bike home while I took all the safety courses and got my motorcycle permit. I've always been very conscious about being safe even though I'm a natural adrenaline junkie and a risk taker. I am a banker, after all; so the risks I took were educated ones and calculated. I took every safety course I could, and I wanted to learn everything about street motorcycle riding. When I finally had my new driver's license with my coveted motorcycle endorsement, I put it in my new Harley wallet which was attached to a chain that drooped around the outside of my hip and attached to the new Harley keychain latched to the front left loop of my prized new studded-leather Harley belt.

Then it was go time.

Back in the day, we lived in Draper, in the southeast foothills of Salt Lake City. We now jokingly like to call it "suburgatory," as we've since moved downtown to the Avenues. We've become urban snobs who don't like to go farther south than our very diverse "live, work, and play" area known as "9th and 9th." But Draper was really a great place to live and raise kids back in our childrearing days. Our children still talk about how much fun they had there, with tons of friends and family time on our boat. Our Draper house was twice as big as our Avenues home, with all the amenities: pool table, ping pong, foosball, card room, theater, hot tub, trampoline, and a wide open sloping mountain hill behind our backyard. It was paradise for our children and our 110-pound golden retriever, Polo, the best pooch ever. Some of our grandkids still call us Grandma and Grandpa Polo, even though he passed on to his next adventure years ago.

The streets in Draper were steep, but I was ready. I was on my new Harley in our driveway, with the family watching, helmet on (safety first), and itching for my first ride. I pulled in the clutch with my left hand, made sure the transmission was in neutral, and with a hard push and then a slight lift of the gear lever with my left foot, I gave the accelerator a bit of gas. I turned my right wrist downward toward the ground, and then pushed the "magic" starter button with my left thumb.

The classic Harley *pop-pop rumble* was immediate, and the serious vibration on the seat was intense. This was before Sportster engines were rubber mounted, so I felt all the energy generated by the powerful Harley V-twin engine sitting just beneath my cheeks. Yeah, those cheeks. I opened the throttle a few more times to let my neighbors know Greg just got a new toy for graduation and that my school days were over for summer—check that—forever! And Greg's ride was good and loud. Fraga, my next-door neighbor, grinned because he appreciated machinery, and also (though I didn't know it at the time) because he was about to buy an even louder "straight-piped" Indian motorcycle, which would light up the entire south end of the valley—and my Harley was his "ticket" to ride.

I looked for traffic, saw the normal slough of neighborhood kids chasing after each other, pushed my left foot down on the peg to engage first gear, and slowly let out the clutch. The Harley and I were one, and the rush was instantaneous. I pulled out onto Wild Hay Lane (and no, we didn't build on this street by accident). Second gear was next, and then a turn to the right, third gear, followed by some fun left turns; fourth gear and then fifth; and I was *gone*. The wind was in my face, and I felt the thrill and sense of freedom that comes with getting rubber on the road and putting the hammer down.

It didn't take long for Laura to get tired of riding behind me. She's a tomboy at heart, and if there's going to be risk-taking and adrenaline ahead, it's going to be on her terms. As her partner and best friend, I knew this day was coming fast. So, like me, she took every safety course offered and got her motorcycle license. I upgraded to a Harley Ultra, its largest "dresser," which is a touring motorcycle with a fairing (a hard, sleek shell covering the front of the bike), windshield, saddle bags, and a comfortable seat that rested against a hard-case trunk. It was like a BarcaLounger on wheels. Then the white Sportster with red sparkling eyes was all Laura's, just waiting to have her mark of right-brained creativity stamped on its keister. Over the course of the next decade, we rode *thousands* of miles together. We both upgraded to Harley Davidson's 100th anniversary edition bikes in 2003. Laura bought a Low Rider and I purchased a classic Heritage Springer. If you have to ask why, you haven't owned a Harley. As they say, "It's not about the destination, it's about the ride."

2

When Laura and I met Jimmy, we immediately connected over our shared love of motorcycles. And since he was a corporate pilot and I loved flying my friends planes, we instantly bonded. He talked about doing the Lolo Pass ride when we partied with our biker friends. It's a huge destination for motorcyclists. A 99-mile strip of Idaho road, passing through the Bitterroot range of the northern Rocky Mountains.

So, on Friday, August 12, 2011, Laura, Jimmy, and I left for a motorcycle trip through Utah and Idaho, on breathtaking back country roads. We'd had motorcycle adventures across the western US, but had yet to immerse ourselves in the canyons of Northern Idaho. The plan was to head north through Utah and Idaho, cut briefly into Montana and pick up Highway 12 in Lolo (just a few miles southwest of Missoula). From there we'd shoot almost due west across Idaho, over the Lolo Pass and through the Clearwater National Forest. Once we reached Lewiston, which is near the border of Idaho and Washington, we'd head due north on Highway 95 up to Coeur d'Alene, Idaho.

Laura and I rode our own separate Harley's, which we'd each became "one" with after many years of motorcycling. Laura was on her custom Low Rider, which admittedly was cooler than my overgrown new Ultra. Mine was more up-to-date, but hers was sportier and much more fun to ride. But, unlike me, she didn't have five different ways to listen to music and Yankee games on Sirius or get to ride on a soft, comfortable lounge seat. Laura had tricked out her Harley with "one off" (i.e., custom-built) chrome daisy wheels, low profile tires, a red leather Corbin seat, and raised handle bars. Her ride fit her like she was born on it.

Jimmy was on his favorite BMW touring bike and probably thought he was more hip than us. Harleys might not be as light or have all the bells and whistles that BMWs do, but they're stronger, meaner, and have twice the value and reputation than any other motorcycle made on the planet. But, Jimmy already knew that, since he switched between Harleys and BMWs constantly. Jimmy's quirkiness is what makes him so much fun to be around.

We covered hundreds of miles on that trip, but the most amazing part of the ride was through the Lolo Pass, which is one of the country's most incredible biker journeys. At the mouth of the pass, we saw several road signs warning of extreme turns and elevation changes. We're from Utah and not strangers to riding severe mountain roads, so we thought, "no biggie." Park rangers and bikers also warned us there were no services through the Pass. In my mind, these warnings were all beckoning us, daring us, calling us—and yes, we answered. "Hells yeah!" Most of our life's activities were based on dares, and our Danish Viking forefathers knew we would say yes before we arrived.

We screamed through the Lolo Pass entrance and were on our way along 99 miles of winding mountain road, not a gas station or Starbucks in sight, and we could chuck our cell phones because we were "off the grid." It felt like we'd left civilization and were instantly on a north country adventure with Lewis and Clark over 200 years ago, covering their same trail through the Idaho Rocky Mountains. The rivers in the Pass were wider and clearer than we had ever seen before at this elevation. The views were jaw-dropping.

Once we reached the Clearwater River, it turned into a real adventure. As we rode beside the rivers in the Clearwater National Forest, there were pine trees and aspens as far as the eyes could see. We passed several fly fishermen standing thigh deep, knowing their only worry was whether to tie on the "pale morning dun" or "golden stonefly." The warm sunshine was glinting off the cool water, and the pine needles, scrub oak leaves, and fresh bark were giving off a scent that only a biker could absorb in every microscopic skin pore and sensory node and truly understand. The idyllic Harley picture was complete.

The Lolo Pass is a very technical ride, with thousand-foot rises and drops in elevation, and winding roads that require constant attention. Some of the curves are tight enough to require dropping back to 15 miles per hour. Personally, I was comfortable on the bike and felt no anxiety about the ride. But what I wasn't comfortable with was watching Laura.

Laura had a Harley accident in 2003; luckily, though her bike was totaled, she was wearing a helmet and she walked away with just bumps and bruises (and a wicked black eye). After that, she always had a hard time with left-hand turns. I'd taken to riding in the "tailgunner" position—last guy in line, back of the pack—so I could keep an eye on her. But her anxiety about turns was always on my mind. It was always on her mind. Unfortunately, her turning anxiety was getting progressively worse over time. In fact, we'd almost sold the bikes a few months before going on this Lolo Pass trip. A huge "beni" of riding with Jimmy was that he didn't care about keeping up a high rate of speed. We were good to go at a pace Laura felt comfortable with, which, at the end of the day, meant everything. It helped decrease Laura's turning anxiety, and it eased my fear of losing what was most important in my life— my best friend, my lover, my wife.

We took it slow and easy, and pulled off to the side of the road often to see the sights (and to give our keisters a rest from the bike seats). The 99-mile stretch of road took all day, and though it was an unforgettable ride, I was sure glad when we pulled into the resort near Kooskia, Idaho, the first sign of civilization in a hundred miles. You could buy something from the convenience store and put gas in the tank.

We were beat. It had been an incredible day, but we were ready for a shower and some dinner. The resort was packed with other likeminded travelers enjoying the Lolo Pass, and we were lucky to get one of their log cabins. The cabin was right next to the wide, soothing Lochsa River.

We went through our normal end-of-day biker routine. We unpacked our bikes and threw our bags on the floor next to our bed. Next job was spraying down our bikes to clean off all the bugs, grime, and road tar. Then it was chrome-polishing time. Grab the Harley chrome spray and fine polishing cloth. And, before we knew it, with a little elbow grease and chemical magic, our bikes were shining like the Goddesses they were meant to be.

But wait, we couldn't forget to clean ourselves after an all-day ride—that's right, we were ripe as all get out! After seeing and riding past the rivers all day long, with the sun beating down on us, we just had to get in and try out that clear, clean water firsthand. It wasn't unusual for Laura and I to hop out of our clothes and take a skinny-dip during a long ride when it was 100-plus degrees—like we did in the Redwood Forest on highway 1 in California—but we kept it PG-rated this time. We dug out our shorts and tanks and jumped in the river. Damn, it felt good to finally get in the water we'd been drooling over all day.

Then, a quick shower and a shave and some appropriate clothes for being seen in public. Bikers pack light, with just two or three bags (not suitcases). Our bags were at least two feet deep, with a flapped opening at the top, and were made of thick, waterproof, heavy, ballistic nylon. They had tie-down straps to keep them secured to the bike while riding. And believe me, you do not want your bag flying off the back of your bike during a ride—it could hit another biker, or a car. And anything that we purchased on the ride would have to find another little secure storage spot. Laura had bought a colorful bag of gumballs for the grandkids that we tucked into the trunk of my bike.

So, after being smooshed into a ball and tied as tightly as possible to the back of a bike all day, our clothes were basically a wrinkled-up brick at the bottom of a rabbit hole. So, digging down to find respectable dinner clothes was not an easy task. Whew... I dried off, slapped on some baby fresh deodorant, sprayed on some Fierce cologne, crammed some gel into what's left of my hair, and then put on what I'd dug out of the bottom of my ballistic vessel.

I was good to go, and it was time to eat.

The resort had a diner on site, and it was packed too. We sat down to peruse the menus, reliving the motorcycle ride in conversation—just like the other riders in the diner were doing. When I saw trout on the menu, I knew I had to have it. I love fish, and after a day spent watching fishermen in the river, it sounded like the perfect meal.

Now, I have to say, I've never been a picky eater. I grew up as one of six kids, and my mom was not the best cook. She was an amazing baker, but dinner time was an adventure. She served us liver and creamed *everything*, all of it overcooked. My parents grew up during the Depression, and their taste showed it. My dad's favorite food was a head of lettuce and sardines. I loved eating snacks with him. We bonded during those moments when I was young. Those were my first memories of living life on a dare—if he offered it to me, I would eat it. So, I grew up eating stuff that tasted weird, and I learned to eat what I was given.

All that to say, I knew from the first bite that the trout didn't taste exactly right, but...the way I was raised, when you went to a restaurant and ordered food, you were meant to eat what came out. Plus, I was starving. So, I slathered on the tartar sauce and just kept going.

I shouldn't have eaten that fish.

3

The next morning, August 15th, was a warm and sunny day. We stopped for breakfast in Kamiah, at a wood-paneled diner plastered with Budweiser signage.

But, to be honest, I don't really remember that. I'm just telling you what I've seen in photos, and what Laura and Jimmy have relayed to me. Looking at the photos, and hearing their stories, I try to connect the dots of what happened that day. There's a photo of me and Laura at the table. We've got blue mugs and half-eaten plates in front of us. I see french toast covered in syrup. Hash brown potatoes. Triangles of toast next to those little jelly containers with the peel-back foil lids. We've got our leather motorcycle jackets hanging off the backs of our red vinyl chairs. A couple of bikers, just taking in some breakfast before a long day of riding. But if I ate anything, I sure don't remember. I can tell you, though, that looking at myself in the photos, I don't look right. I was ... off. Laura and Jimmy later told me that I was in and out of the bathroom all morning, though I have only a vague memory of that.

A few hours later, we'd made it to the Lewiston Highway 95 interchange. We stopped to fill our tanks and rest before another long stretch. We were headed a hundred-plus miles up to Coeur d'Alene on highway 95. Another photo from that day shows me sitting on my bike in the shade, holding a bottle of 7-Up. Looking at that, I know I must have been feeling that trout rearing its ugly head. That one was straight out of mom's home remedies—if you're feeling sick to your stomach, drink 7-Up.

We were having a bit of a rest—Laura was making some business calls; Jimmy was on his phone. So, that left me with my phone too.

I remember sitting on my bike, texting our kids to say "I love you." Now, I love our children, for sure—I've always been affectionate and demonstrative with them and our grandkids. But this texting was unusual; it wasn't typically something that would come to mind while Laura and I were in the midst of an adventure. I'd usually be totally immersed in the moment, focused on the adrenaline rush. But for some reason I felt like I needed to text the kids right then. So, inexplicably, I found myself in a gas station parking lot, sitting on my bike in the middle of Idaho, drinking a 7-Up and expressing my love.

I wouldn't see their replies for several weeks. Jimmy and Laura were ready to roll, so I put my phone away, pulled out of the convenience store behind Jimmy and Laura, and headed north on 95.

And that was it—my last memory until I found myself in Intermountain Medical Center eleven days later.

4

For the first couple hours, our ride was uneventful. We rode north on 95 through Moscow and the Saint Joe national forest. The weather had taken a turn toward chilly rain, and so we pulled over a few times to put on our protective gear—leather chaps, padded leather jackets, long gloves—to keep us warm and dry as we rode the rain-slicked two-lane road. Being all about safety, I wore my brand-new Harley ultra-light half helmet, which I liked because it didn't give me the dreaded helmet headache. Laura and Jimmy wore full face helmets. They both told me they asked multiple times if I was okay because I kept having to pull over to use the bathroom, but I assured them I was. We were so close to Coeur d'Alene, I probably didn't want to stop. Part of the bikers' code is that it's always your own decision whether to ride. No. One. Else's.

We made a stop yet again to put on more gear, and I took over the "road boss" position at the front of the pack. I hardly ever rode front. After Laura's accident, I almost always rode behind her to make sure she was safe. Road Boss was not a comfortable place for me. I don't know why I took the lead. Enigma.

* * *

At 1:30 in the afternoon, about thirty miles south of Coeur d'Alene, I signaled to pull over and slowed down from sixty miles per hour to about thirty. I rode the white line for a moment and Laura, riding behind me, wondered if I was going to stop or if I'd readjust and keep going. She was probably thinking *what the hell?* We'd been stopping every thirty to sixty minutes for the last two hours to go to the bathroom or put on more rain gear. She was probably thinking we should just stop for the night. But I wanted to keep going. We were so close to Coeur d'Alene, we could almost smell it.

Then Laura saw my head droop to the side and rest on my right shoulder—and then she watched me pass out.

"NO!"

My body went limp and fell to the right, forcing my bike to veer off the road, down the gravel embankment, toward a ditch filled with lava rocks. According to Laura, it appeared that I only passed out for a few seconds, but it might as well have been several lifetimes. She saw me holding onto the handle bars like I was trying to regain control. Jimmy said I hit the lava rocks, which sent me airborne across the ditch. My Ultra weighed over a thousand pounds loaded up with gas, all my gear, plus a bit over two hundred pounds of me. Flying it with both wheels off the ground would have taken horrendous speed and lift. I must have held on to the bars and gripped that sucker between my legs tighter than any Thighmaster, giving Suzanne Somers a run for her money. Laura told me later that I had bruises along my entire inner legs. It must have taken a Herculean effort to keep from being thrown from that bike. I don't remember a damn thing.

I scorched through the grassy hill, parallel to the ditch, down the mountainside. The fun and games were over. If I could remember what was coming next, I can only imagine it would have been the ultimate adrenaline rush. Good thing I don't.

It was go time. A downhill Olympic ski run. Only I didn't have skis, or a safe landing zone like at the Utah Olympic Park ski jump. A three-foot drop-off leading back into the ditch, covered with sharp black lava rock tips, glaring up at me as if to say, "I dare you, bro." But there was no ramp, just a screaming taunt.

Reaching a ledge would normally send dopamine coursing throughout my synapses with a full-on cliff jumping thrill—but only when it's a calculated risk, and this was anything but. I reached the edge, riding over tall blades of wild turf that gleamed under a fresh coat of rain. There was no going back.

Drop off. A brief moment of no tension, a millisecond of free fall, and then...

* * *

I met the lava rocks head on, crashing the front tire and wheel cover, and within a moment the Ultra began its descent into destruction. The right wheel housing and cover collapsed, and the right engine guard was next. What makes the Ultra unique is that its engine guard holds two small plastic fairings and glove boxes for your gear, conveniently within reach on long rides. The right glove box and fairing were instantly ripped off and pulverized into pieces. Out burst a variety of odds and ends: eye drops, CDs, fingerless gloves, and a spray bottle of glass cleaner for my visor. The impact forced the release of my travel bag and the remaining contents of my trunk, and the white hard-case saddlebag at my side was smashed, its lid torn off. Their contents exploded over the accident site. In an instant, my belongings became wreckage. Two identical six-inch pieces of the white front fairing were destined to find a new home, driven into the earth by the force of the Ultra's oncoming thousand-pound thrust. They stuck together, as if they were meant to be laid to rest, memorializing the crash site. RIP G's Harley Ultra fairing partners. Until we meet again. A lava rock marked their final resting place.

The shiny hardened-steel right engine guard had its own mission. Its target was me. Given that the force of impact was great enough to bend it inward despite its strength and bulk, you can only imagine the fate of my right leg. The engine guard crushed it against an unyielding Harley V-twin engine and wreaked havoc on every tender living element between my hip and big toe.

Above my helmet visor was the right side of my forehead, as yet untouched and innocently hanging out, its executive function trying to wake me up and take control of my brain's input of this devastating moment. It didn't know it was about to take on the fullest extent of the savagery of the crash. A single lava rock sat firmly in bed with its brothers, unaware it was about to play a starring role in the rest of my life. When my head hit the ground, the rock's galvanized point was in my way. A dime-sized diameter doesn't seem like much until the power of speed and weight is forced against it.

The collision instantly sent shockwaves through my brain, setting off a chain reaction that took control of everything I once knew. Grey matter was set in motion, smashing against the interior of my skull. The internal trauma within my head had its own momentum and trajectory. The violence was horrific.

My Harley landed on top of me, its final crushing blow pulverizing me into the lava bed. I was entangled in its grasp. When the dust settled, my right hand was upward a bit, leaning against the throttle, as if it were motioning, "I'm trying to hang on by a thread here, world!" Maybe the crash didn't happen exactly like this; what did I know, anyway? All I knew for sure was that, from that moment on, I was in my safe place. Knocked out with no sense of what had happened to me.

* * *

The ordeal was over by the time Laura put down her kickstand.

Immediately, she and Jimmy jumped into action. They hadn't actually witnessed the culmination of the crash because Laura had been focused on not crashing her own bike. She kept telling herself, "I can't crash again. I can't crash again. I need to stop slowly and put my kickstand down. I need to put my kickstand down." She was in shock from watching me pass out and ride into the ditch. Jimmy pulled up behind Laura and got off his BMW.

They immediately came running to find me unconscious, pinned under the bike. This put them both into panic mode. Their first action was getting the behemoth off me. Immediately, she grabbed the Ultra's handlebars while Jimmy grabbed the back seat and fender. They didn't talk. Didn't need to. Laura was thinking, "I need to just lift, lean, and push this freakin' VW bus off of you and push it over to the road so I can take care of you." Adrenaline rushed in their veins as they lifted the damaged Ultra upright on its tires and pushed it over toward the road. Laura and Jimmy are heroes.

Not only was I unconscious, but my right leg was twisted at the knee at an angle you wouldn't want to look at, and blood oozed through gashes in my black leather chaps. Fortunately, since Lara was an EMT she knew what to do. She covered me with a blanket to prevent me from going into shock. She positioned herself around my head stabilizing my neck as best as she could as she sat on the sharp lava bed. Laura held onto my shoulders so she could roll me to the side slightly when needed so I wouldn't aspirate my vomit. She saved my life.

Since there was no cellular service in the area, Jimmy got back on his bike and found his way to higher ground where he could call for help.

Seeing the accident, motorists and bikers pulled over to help. As luck would have it, after about fifteen minutes, two of the travelers who stopped were a doctor and a nurse. They put on gloves and jumped in to help. Laura stayed and cradled my head. They assured her that she was taking all the right measures. They assisted with the EMT work.

Laura saved me on that bed of lava rocks and kept me alive while we waited for Life Flight and paramedics. I would have died and gone on to my next adventure in a matter of minutes without her.

An ambulance showed up, and EMTs isolated my neck and lifted me out of the rocks and onto a backboard. They carried me to the ambulance. I screamed uncontrollably and thrashed around so wildly that they had to wrap my hands together with duct tape so I wouldn't hurt myself. Beyond that, there was no more the EMTs could do until Life Flight arrived so paramedics could attend to me. I was unresponsive other than screaming from the pain. I cried out irrationally, yelling repetitive incoherent phrases—like, "Come on, Richie!" (I still don't know who the hell Richie might be...)

Laura couldn't help me anymore, and my screaming had exploded her emotional control. She stood on the side of the road, away from the ambulance, with Jimmy, anxiously wondering what was happening and where Life Flight was. As they waited, Laura noticed that the grassy hillside was dotted with colorful orbs. The gumballs. She sat there listening to me scream, she looked out, mesmerized, at the scattered gumballs marking the pathway of my flight across the gleaming grassy knoll. The lid of my Harley trunk case had been ejected on impact during my first airborne ditch-jump, giving the gumballs their freedom.

* * *

Life Flight was contacted at 1:47pm and landed around 2:20pm at the accident scene. Two crew members, a paramedic and a registered nurse, rushed into the ambulance. Ideally, Life Flight sets down, puts the patient on their gurney, loads it in the helicopter, and they take off to the nearest trauma hospital. Instead, this critical care team landed and turned off the helicopter because they had serious work on their hands to stabilize me and get me prepped for the ride. The road, which had become a temporary helipad, had to be shut down by the Idaho Highway Patrol and two sheriff patrol cars from different towns.

Later, looking at the notes from the Life Flight crew and Kootenai Health ER, I know that they were delayed because I was combative, irrational, and had obvious "decreased mental status." My coma rating was severe, initially an eight on the Glasgow scale. I was "near unintelligible," and I had "no recall." I couldn't obey commands, answer questions, or open my eyes. They had to cut off my thick leather riding gear to get a fuller picture of my injuries. The ridiculously expensive Harley jacket—it had cost close to a thousand dollars—was shredded without a thought.

And just like that, the shiny bike and the gear and the accessories, all of those physical representations of my love of adventure, all of which seemed so fundamental to who I was and the life Laura and I had created together—*gone.*

Upon first inspection, it was clear I had a large hematoma—a clot of broken blood vessels—on the right side of my forehead where I'd had the unfortunate meeting with the lava rock. I had severe respiratory failure. My right leg and knee were swollen, and I had long lacerations down my shin and a damaged foot. The paramedics suspected a severe traumatic brain injury due to my coma rating, but of course that would take time to diagnose for certain.

It took four people to restrain me so they could get an IV into my arm, after which they immediately pumped me full of medicine—they induced paralysis so they could intubate me to keep me breathing and keep me from thrashing and hurting myself. They also gave me sedatives, painkillers, and anti-anxiety medicine. They worked feverishly on the ground to revive my stats and get my breathing pattern stabilized so I could withstand the flight.

Finally, after thirty minutes—though it seemed like forever to Laura and Jimmy—the medics transferred me to the aircraft stretcher and moved me into the helicopter. Jimmy talked the helicopter pilot into letting Laura fly with me. It was a very small helicopter and they had me positioned in the right front nose area, feet first. Laura sat in the middle by my head. We took off at 2:50pm.

Almost immediately, they couldn't get the electronic ventilator to work, so they had to "bag" me by hand to keep oxygen flowing into my lungs. This worried Laura. The paramedic was busy doing everything she could to keep me stabilized, so Laura volunteered to help. For the duration of the flight, Laura bagged me every four seconds. Can you imagine? Every *four* seconds of a *thirty*-minute flight, my wife breathed for me. I would have been brain dead without her.

During flight, the crew contacted the emergency room at Kootenai Health in Coeur d'Alene to give them my status and their ETA. A code "red" was announced in the ER and throughout the hospital, and critical physicians were notified. Through an act of sheer serendipity, one of the travelers stuck at the roadblock at the accident site was the brother-in-law of Dr. Bowen, the orthopedic surgeon at Kootenai who'd soon be tasked with putting my demolished body back together. Dr. Bowen's brother-in-law took a picture of the accident site and Life Flight and texted him to let him know he had an incoming critical patient. Everything was set and Kootenai's ER and Critical Care team was ready for me.

In the medical world, there's a term—the "golden hour"—to describe the precious window of time during which medical intervention is crucial in giving the trauma victim a fighting chance at survival. The first responders who helped Laura save my life at the crash site were heroic men and women who got me through that golden hour. They put their lives on the line to save a stranger who was passing through town on a Harley ride.

When we landed on the roof helipad at 3:20pm, two hospital staffers met the helicopter. They, along with the Life Flight medics and Laura, wheeled me from the "H" along an elevated pathway to a small shed where the elevator was. At this point, Laura was in shock and her post-traumatic stress disorder had already begun to develop. The flight had seemed to take forever, and she had no idea what town we'd even landed in because she'd been so focused on bagging me. Everything looked incredibly small. Too small to do the type of critical medical work she thought I was about to need. But there was nothing she could do but go with it, holding on to the railing of the gurney as they wheeled me toward the ER. There, doctors and nurses awaited me—gloves on and hands up.

5

A horde of physicians and critical care personnel immediately took charge, working all around me to get me connected to a myriad of machines and get an up-to-the-second picture of my vitals, assessing the paramedics' reports and comparing them relative to my current state. It was a dire situation. I was still intubated and hooked up to the ventilator, as well as other machines that monitored my oxygen and blood. The ER team completed their initial assessments of the severity of my head and leg injuries, and the lead neurology and orthopedic surgeons were on their way. They ordered a rush on CT scans and x-rays. This whole time, Laura stayed by my bed in the small examination room, sitting on a white plastic chair, holding my hand. There were so many medical people that when they needed to come by she had to move back against the wall to create two or three feet of room for them to get through.

At first, the hum of activity and the efficiency and competence of the ER staff made Laura feel relieved that I was being taken care of in a good hospital. The staff was very comforting and calmly communicated their procedures. Laura hoped they'd be able to fix me soon and we could go home. But when Laura saw how many members of the critical care staff were arriving—including a chaplain and a social worker—she grew alarmed. It was dawning on her just how complex and severe my injuries must be.

And then the onslaught of inquiries started. The neurosurgeon, Dr. William Ganz, took Laura into the hallway outside my ER room and grilled her with questions—about the accident, my medical history, and my medications. She started getting nervous because she couldn't answer them all. If she wasn't in a state of shock she'd have remembered to inform Dr. Ganz that this was not my first Traumatic Brain Injury rodeo.

The first TBI I sustained was when I was in high school trying to keep up with my friends on a black diamond run at Alta Ski Resort. I crashed and landed myself in the hospital. My second TBI happened when I was in my 20s racing bicycles in England. I took the lead heading downhill and didn't make the turn at the bottom. Most of the bones on the left side of my face were broken.

Dr. Ganz was in an understandably tense situation. Laura was waiting for help from our doctor in Salt Lake, but the answers weren't coming fast enough. The weight was on Dr. Ganz's shoulders to determine the extent of my brain injury and decide on the most expedient neurological procedure to save my life and give me the best chance to recover at the highest level of brain function possible. When Laura couldn't answer his questions, he was understandably frustrated. He was running out of time. He quickly turned around to go back into my room and assess my state. He requested more exams.

When Dr. Ganz came back out to speak to Laura again, she finally asked where we were. When he told her we were at Kootenai Medical Center in Coeur d'Alene, Laura insisted, "We can't stay here! Please, fly us back home to Salt Lake City. We have a brand-new hospital there, and they'll know how to take care of Greg." Dr. Ganz said, "If we were going to fly Greg anywhere, it would be Seattle, but he won't make it there. He won't survive a flight anywhere." Dr. Ganz left quickly, knowing he didn't have time for this—my life was hanging in the balance.

The tense questioning, the number of critical care physicians, and the obvious urgency of the medical procedures—it finally put Laura in overwhelm. She reached her limit. Distraught, she fell against the wall and sank to the floor, sobbing. She was alone. A stranger in a distant city. She was in shock and experiencing severe post-traumatic stress.

Dr. Bowen, my orthopedic surgeon, watched the exchange between Laura and Dr. Ganz. He cringed as he watched her drop to the floor. She was visibly broken. He walked over to Laura and tenderly helped her up and led her to an empty ER room to try to calm her. It was Dr. Bowen's brother-in-law who had texted a picture from the crash site. He assured Laura that Dr. Ganz was one of the best neurosurgeons in the country. What we didn't know at the time was that Dr. Bowen had recently lost his father to a fatal head injury from a snowmobile accident, so he keenly related to Laura's extreme distress. "You've gotta trust me, Laura," Dr. Bowen said. "If it were one of my family members in Greg's situation, I would choose Dr. Ganz."

Despite what may have seemed to Laura like harsh grilling, Dr. Ganz was in the incredibly difficult position of having to make split-second decisions on bad information. He didn't know me, my medical history, or what medicines I was taking, and yet every minute he had to make and re-make the decision about whether to operate. Every second mattered, especially within the critical first twenty-four hours after a traumatic brain injury. His sole mission was to get the most accurate information possible so he could save a life. My life. A neurosurgeon in an intense moment like this can't be hindered by emotion or held up by hurt feelings. You wouldn't give him marks for bedside manner, but he's the guy to go to if you want to get your life saved. He questioned Laura, even though she was in the midst of her own trauma, and when he got the information he needed, he had to walk away and do the work.

This left Laura to deal, all alone, with her emotions. This was her first time in Coeur d'Alene and she didn't know anyone. Laura's anguish was unbearable. Dr. Bowen's gentleness and timing were perfect, but then she was ushered into the waiting room of the intensive care unit on the second floor. An important thing to know about Laura is that she doesn't wait. Waiting is not in her DNA. So, waiting for the answers or for bad news would have put Laura in a disastrous state. I would not have wanted to be the person to cross her while waiting for Dr. Ganz to give her my diagnosis.

A social worker noticed Laura in the ICU waiting room, sitting alone with her arms wrapped around herself, still wearing all of her Harley gear—covered in mud, my vomit, and my blood. Knowing that Laura was waiting for Dr. Ganz, the social worker sat down next to her and asked how she was doing. She offered to help Laura get out of her motorcycle gear. Laura thanked the woman but turned down the help. She was reluctant to take off her gear because a part of her thought that if she could just keep it on, the doctors would tell her I was okay and that we could just go home. Taking off the gear would be like admitting that I was badly injured and facing a lengthy hospital stay.

In the meanwhile, an ER physician performed surgery to insert a line catheter (called a peripherally inserted central catheter, or PIC line) through my chest to a vein near my heart for central distribution of medications. This whole time, Dr. Ganz was holding off on cutting into my brain. There were two options—either the medicine would reduce the swelling and bleeding, or he'd have to drill into my head or slice a piece of my skull to relieve the pressure. He had to constantly judge which medications to use, and at what dosages, all without knowing for sure what meds I might already be on and whether they'd possibly interact poorly. If medications couldn't control the swelling and bleeding, then it would be into brain surgery. That's risky. The outcome is never sure. There's just no way of knowing what a person's cognitive function is going to be afterward.

The most critical element of my situation was the midline shift. The bleeding and swelling in my brain was severe, pushing my brain off-center. It was strange because the primary impact of my crash was on my right forehead. That damn lava rock drove its point into the right side of my helmet, just above my visor. Due to my brain ricocheting off the inside of my skull, my traumatic brain injury was on the opposite side of impact—my left hemisphere–the same area as my two previous TBIs. There's a certain degree of midline shift that makes brain surgery an inevitability, and I was right on the edge.

And Laura, all she could do was wait—she'd already waited onsite at the scene of the accident, listening to me scream, and now she was waiting at the ICU. Compounding Laura's fear and pain was that she couldn't help but think of her mother's death from a glioblastoma brain tumor at age sixty-one. Her mom had been a neuro ICU nurse, and though her neurosurgeon wanted to perform a biopsy, Laura's mom knew the biopsy was risky and there was a high likelihood she wouldn't be able to communicate after they performed it. She'd seen it before in patients. And that's exactly what happened. The procedure damaged her brain, left her unconscious and unable to speak, thus confirming the diagnosis. She only lived one more week. This was top of mind for Laura the whole time she was hearing Dr. Ganz weigh the options for me. She thought that if they could save me without operating on my brain, I'd have a fighting chance of returning to normal eventually and everything would be okay. Compounding Laura's shock and PTSD, she was worried that if they cut into my skull, she'd never be able to communicate with me again.

At this early stage, Laura was all by herself at the hospital, with no friends or family around—Jimmy was off taking care of getting my demolished bike to Spokane's Harley dealership and coordinating a way to have one of his friends ride Laura's bike home to Salt Lake. Finally, she let the social worker help her take off her Harley jacket, vest, and chaps and put the disgusting leathers into a bag. I can't imagine the smell. My vomit. My blood. All mixed with dirt, sweat, and tears.

Even though I was the guy in the coma, Laura's trauma was more severe than mine. I don't have any memories of the accident or the physical trauma. Laura does. She saw everything, heard everything, and remembers everything. While I had a trove of medical professionals looking after me, she was all alone, making life-altering decisions for us both, in a pressure-cooker situation. The truth of it is, it wasn't just me and my bike that went into that ditch; in ways, Laura came with us. From that moment on, she was forced into a role she didn't ask for and sure as hell didn't want or deserve: the role of caretaker for a traumatic brain injury survivor. And I put her there.

6

Wile Laura was riding through hell, waiting for some sort of definitive news from the doctors, I was having a very different experience. Given the severity of my injuries and the physical agony I must have been experiencing, you'd probably think I was having a pretty bad time. But what I actually felt could only be described as bliss.

Yes, bliss.

Language falls short of what I'm about to describe, so I can only offer an approximation of the experience. But during all the urgent medical procedures and frantic worry on the part of Laura and Jimmy, I was in a quiet, blissful place; a realm that was adjacent to the reality I was accustomed to being in, but void of any pain or fear. It was an experience that had no beginning or end, and while in it, I felt like I was floating in an ocean, surrounded by boundless warmth and love that sprung from an endless source. I was told later that my body was going through absolute agony, twisted in places it shouldn't have been, and that my wounds were ghastly. Parts of my brain had been destroyed. I was mostly silent other than short periods of murmuring and talking nonsense. But while those may have been the facts of the matter, it was not my experience of it. I knew there was medical "stuff" happening around me—I could sense the people and the equipment and the frantic activity— but I didn't know that I was part of it or that it had anything to do with me. I could acknowledge it, but it was irrelevant to my experience. I didn't know that I was close to death. I didn't *know* anything other than I was at complete peace.

I occupied a space that was all energy, nothing short of energy. I've struggled to find words in the English language to describe this; all the words available to me seem too superficial. I suppose the term that comes closest is "near-death experience," though there was no white light or long tunnel like you might imagine. Instead, my experience was one of profound spiritual connection with the people around me. When Laura sat next to me and held my hand, I was internally connected with her. I could feel all that she was. I was her and she was me. There was no separation. I could feel her as if I *were* her. It was pure experience. Laura and I are really close, but these were emotions I'd never experienced at anywhere near this depth; I could feel her love, hope, joy, peace, and companionship. I was in direct contact with her most intimate desires for me. And yet, at the same time, I was blocked from every negative thought and feeling she was having. She was scared to death for me, but that didn't come through. I got to experience, for the first time in my life, the absence of negativity. Usually life is so obscured by worry and fear. And without anxiety, which I usually experience in extremely high doses, I got to experience a bliss state—a state that *could* be the day-to-day human experience if we were able to let go of our perceived separation.

Later, Laura told me everything she did to save my life at the crash site, in that sharp bed of lava rocks. But she really saved me through our internal connection. Her hope and courage, which were constant within me throughout my coma, were the dynamic energy forces that ultimately saved my life and drove my recovery.

7

When the medical team was finally able to get a full accounting of all the damage, the news was pretty damn bad. I was incredibly banged up. I had many broken bones and lacerations, but it was my head that took the brunt of the crash. My traumatic brain injury (or TBI) was something called a "coup contrecoup." For those of you who like the gory details, here's what happened. When the right side of my forehead crammed, at highway speed, into the point of that lava rock, the impact caused my skull to temporarily bend inward, striking my brain. This set my mainframe's hardware into motion at the same speed of my bike, knocking my brain into the interior of the other side of my skull. This resulted in a TBI on the left hemisphere of my brain between my forehead and temple. The initial CT scans showed a subdural hematoma—bleeding into the space between the brain and the dura (the brain covering)—from vein tears on my left frontal lobe. The hematoma was visible across the left side of my brain and back onto my rear occipital lobe. I also had bleeding on my right frontal lobe and a large right scalp hematoma—a ginormous goose egg—on my forehead where I hit the point of the lava rock. Bleeding and swelling caused an increase in intracranial pressure, which resulted in compression and damage to delicate brain tissue in the left portion of my head. An acute subdural hematoma is often life-threatening. Dr. Ganz classified my coma of a "severe" Glasgow rating of a six when I reached the hospital. The combination of acute hematoma and a "severe" Glasgow coma rating of between six and eight results in high mortality rates of fifty to ninety percent (according to UCLA Health Neurosurgery). But mine was diagnosed early at the crash site by the paramedics and in the ER by Dr. Ganz and the critical care team, so there was hope.

The CT scans also revealed traumatic subarachnoid hemorrhages—bleeding inside my brain. Blood was scattered inside my left frontal lobe, across the vertex, and eventually settled in the parietal lobe. The CT scans also showed "mass effect" bleeding into my brain furrows and against my skull. Long story short, there was blood and swelling above and under my skull and bleeding throughout my brain. I was in trouble.

As if that weren't enough, the neurology team was concerned about a severe left-to-right seven-millimeter midline shift of my brain. This shift was the result of bleeding and swelling caused by the subdural hematoma, which put pressure in the left side of my skull. This forced the midline of my cerebrum into the right area of my head. It's really bad when your whole brain is forced into one area of your skull. Like, deadly. When it comes to a midline shift, there is a point of no return where the shift is severe enough to require immediate surgery. Fortunately, I wasn't there yet, but it was damn close—edge-of-the-cliff close. The shift was continually monitored, which required several CT scans and neurology evaluations during those initial hours. Dr. Ganz was constantly monitoring the level of my midline shift, the size of my subdural hematoma, delivering doses of medications trying to stop the increased bleeding and swelling inside my brain and deciding whether to perform brain surgery.

And, mind you, I wasn't just a wreck from the neck up. The impact of the crash had broken the base of my right femur into several segments, and my massive thighbone was driven into my knee. The CT showed vertical fractures through my femoral condyle. The downward force of my femur tore the tendon off my kneecap and forced it into the remaining space on the left side of my knee. I had several comminution fragments—small fractures inside my knee joint. In terms I understand, one of the biggest bones of my body, my femur, was crammed into my knee joint. Since my foot had been on the riding platform of my Ultra, the force of crashing into the ditch hadn't allowed any give for the knee when my thighbone was jammed into it. Result? The impact broke the section of my femur in several places, resulting in a severe "fracture defect," according to Dr. Bowen's charting notes. That's a major injury on its own.

Every action leads to a reaction. The onslaught of the engine guard was next. It smashed my knee joint and lower femur, leaving bits of bone and joint pieces in its wake. As my joint deteriorated, its tendons let loose, dislocating my knee, releasing the pressure that had kept my foot on the Harley's foot platform. As my knee lost its tendon buddies and its connection to my femur, all hell broke loose. My lower right leg was then free from being attached—to me. The lower half of my leg shot off to the right, allowing it free access to the severity of the sharp lava rocks when my Harley finished its flight path and made its descent into a no-landing zone.

The jagged tips of the rocks cut large lacerations down my shin and jammed holes into my lower leg. The crash landing crushed the big toe of my right foot, demolished the bone structure and nearly tore the entire toenail off, despite it being protected under steel-toed riding boots. It was described as a complex comminuted fracture, which means the bones were broken into multiple pieces. The impact also left me with a severely sprained right ankle, caused by stretching of the surrounding ligaments. The palm of my right hand appeared to be deeply bruised, probably from hitting my handlebars or holding on tight to the edge of my grip during the crash. My inner thighs were deeply bruised from impact against the bike as I hung on for dear life as I careened into the ditch.

Later, I got to see the helmet that saved my life. A black Harley ultra-light half helmet adorned with two fierce-looking skulls. It was scraped up and covered in a thin layer of dirt, with a dime-sized dent where I made contact with the lava rock that rocked my brain and my world.

8

Of course, in dire situations like these, you contact one person and it sets the line of dominoes falling...

Jimmy called our son-in-law Brant, who is married to our daughter Jodi. Brant and Jodi were at Costco with their two kids. Of course, Jodi could tell right away that something was wrong, and demanded to know what. So, Brant had to tell her about the crash, right there in the store. She became hysterical. That was the first domino—and we had five more adult children, six grandkids at the time, and lots of extended family, friends, and colleagues, so there were a lot of dominoes. Brant and Jodi called Scott, another of our sons-in-law, and he shared the news with our daughter, Tristen. She's a nurse, and so of course she wanted the medical data, but there wasn't much to share yet—everyone was in limbo, anxiously waiting to see whether I'd be sent in for brain surgery. Tristen contacted our son Josh, who is a sports fanatic and adrenaline junkie like me. He couldn't believe it. He was shocked and fearful. And Josh wasn't easily spooked.

Some of the family was busy and couldn't be reached right away—our son Jeremy was at a play rehearsal and my sister Debbie was at a church event, so their phones were on silent. Two of our kids lived out of town—Jaci lived in Cedar City, and Ryan, who is an officer in the Navy, lived in Virginia Beach and was stationed at Norfolk. No one could get through to any of them. Of course, when they finally checked their phones, they saw all the missed calls and messages and freaked out.

Eventually, after some delays, all friends and family were contacted and brought as up-to-date as anyone could be, given the circumstances. They were frantic, scared, distraught. And many of them wanted to travel to Coeur d'Alene. They wanted something to *do*.

Laura wasn't having it, though. In general, she's fiercely independent and doesn't like to ask for help, and those instincts kicked in *hard*. She tried to turn everyone away. She just wanted to be alone with me. She was anything but her normal self. She was in severe shock and PTSD was now her center. Her stance was, "It's okay. We're only gonna be up here for a minute, and then we'll be home." Jodi had already bought a plane ticket, but Laura forcefully told her to stay home since Jodi had so much on her plate with two kids. Other friends and family had tickets or were on the road up to Coeur d'Alene but were told to stay home. In Laura's mind, my ICU room in Kootenai Health was private and a place where we could be together in healing. Maybe she was feeling a sense of my safe place and the peacefulness of my adjacent sphere.

A few family members did manage to push their way in—our kids Tristen and Josh, and my sister Debbie—but initially Laura didn't like it. She didn't want anything or anyone distracting her focus or coming between us. It didn't occur to her that I needed my family and close friends—their voices, their physical touch, their presence.

Laura had a particularly hard conversation with one of my best friends who I'd known since high school. He and Laura are two peas in a pod—both type-A, take-charge personalities. And in this instance, they clashed horribly. My friend had recently lost his daughter to a head trauma. And he tried to take control of the situation—going so far as to call Dr. Ganz and fib about being my brother in order to get my medical status. He was doing what he thought was best to help Laura and take pressure off her plate, but she really just needed a listening ear. At this point, any pressure, from anyone, put her over the edge. She felt bad about not allowing him to come up to Coeur d'Alene, and she knew he was still in a place of grief over his daughter. It was an awful situation for both of them. I was in my sea of love and had no idea any of this was happening.

Another factor at play was that Laura was scared to death to let my colleagues at the bank know just how bad of shape I was in. She wanted to protect my job. When she called my boss and my bank partner, she gave them the barest information. Laura wanted to control the narrative, and the story she was trying to tell was "Greg's going to be fine." It was a total fiction, of course. My brain had just ricocheted like a pinball inside my skull. I was screwed.

Of course, in hindsight it's easy to see that Laura wasn't thinking straight. How could she have been? She was deep in shock, suffering from intense post-traumatic stress, and was in the nightmare position of making life-or-death decisions on my behalf, in an unfamiliar hospital. She didn't know who to rely upon.

It didn't help matters that everywhere she turned, people wanted to pray for us—even strangers in the waiting room. This was awkward for Laura. She was going through a personal transition in her faith at that time and didn't quite know how to react to all of the religious sentiments. She accepted the well-meaning prayers with gratitude, and she felt the kindness of strangers. But she was also beside herself with grief, and some of the attention read like pressure to her. She felt bombarded. And for better or worse, she initially responded by shutting down and turning herself into an island.

Jimmy and Laura were taking shifts staying with me. At about five in the morning, Jimmy told Laura to get out of there and go lay down, so she went back to Walden House, which is a hospitality center where families can stay to be nearby critically ill or injured patients who are being cared for at Kootenai. After lying down for a few hours, she texted Jimmy to let him know she was up and he said, "Great, I'll bring you a cup of coffee." It was a beautiful day, and they sat outside on the curb in the sunshine, drinking coffee and talking. Comforting each other. Jimmy's cell phone rang and it was the mechanic from the Harley dealership in Spokane. He'd called to tell Jimmy that the Ultra was totaled. When Jimmy mentioned to the mechanic that he was with Laura, the mechanic asked them to hold the phone up so they could both hear him. And then he immediately started saying a prayer for both of them and for me. Laura and Jimmy both just started to sob. Even after they got off the phone, they just sat sobbing and drinking their coffee.

Jimmy said to Laura, "You have to picture this guy. He weighs three hundred pounds, he's got a beard down to his belly button, he's covered in leather Harley gear, and he works on motorcycles. He's a big, burly Harley guy. Nicest guy you'd ever want to meet and here he is on the phone, praying for us."

As they both sat there crying, Laura thought to herself at that moment, "People are so good." It was so unexpected that the mechanic had called for a transaction and then it turned into such a personal moment. It didn't matter that they probably didn't share the same religion. It didn't matter that Laura didn't know exactly what to "do" with the prayers and the attention that left her feeling both grateful and overwhelmed. She was just blown away by a loving, human moment that reminded her that relationships are what it's all about in this world.

9

The team at Kootenai had me in lifesaving mode on day one and midway through day two. But as soon as I was stabilized, they shifted into recovery mode. When the brain is injured, the surrounding healthy tissue kicks into gear to take over the functions of the dead cells. A good analogy is that your brain is like a corporate office; if a coworker suddenly quits their job, other people in the office have to pick up their duties. They probably aren't very good at these new duties at first, but they learn and improve over time. So, that's sort of what's happening in the brain, and to train my newly recruited neurological "coworkers," the team began engaging with my brain the minute I got there. Even when I was in a coma, my primary nurse Chauntae and the other members of my RN neuro ICU team were in the room every hour, asking, "Can you squeeze my hand?" and "what's your name?" and "who are you?" As soon as I woke up and had my oh-so-profound "WTF?" moment on the fourth day of my coma, therapists were hustling me into practicing various speech, occupational, and physical tools. I was going in and out of a coma, but they had to get the healthy portions of my brain jump started again.

My speech pathologist tested my swallowing capabilities right out of the chute since I was no longer intubated and was breathing on my own. Swallowing is critical from a neuro rehab perspective. The brain and stomach are connected neurologically. Chemicals produced by the brain flow through nervous system and into the stomach and intestinal tract. After eating, nutrients are absorbed through the intestines and end up in the brain's neuro system. Neurosurgeons and therapists know it is critical for patients to have high levels of nutrition as early as possible after a traumatic brain injury in order to enhance recovery. Feeding tubes are necessary with coma patients like me. I was getting my nutrition in liquid form, and they had to confirm I could swallow before they could disconnect the feeding tube.

The evening of day two, once Dr. Ganz felt certain that I could handle sedation, Dr. Bowen got the go-ahead to reconstruct my leg. The surgery was so complex and unique, several surgeons watched the surgery as a learning opportunity. Over the course of three and a half hours, Dr. Bowen rebuilt my knee and femur with screws and plates, using his technical orthopedic savvy. He said it was a happy day when he found my kneecap intact in the crevice under where my joint used to be. He moved my kneecap back into place and was able to reattach my tendon with a half screw.

After repairing my broken femur, he reattached it to my knee joint and made sure it was functioning properly. The titanium plates and screws held strong, bracing the base of the femur against my rebuilt knee. That had to have been a proud moment for Dr. Bowen amidst his peers. Against the odds, a replacement knee wasn't needed.

Now it was time for Dr. Bowen to shift his focus to my broken big toe. He took the remaining toenail off so he could realign the busted bones of the toe joints. He then repaired my nail bed and ingeniously sewed my toenail back on as a splint to hold all the repaired pieces together and protect the nail bed. He fixed the long deep cuts down my leg and holes in my shin. After all was said and done, Dr. Bowen told Laura that he was confident that I would walk again with physical therapy.

I made it through the surgery on my leg, but I apparently did my damndest to jeopardize Dr. Bowen's excellent work. One of the upshots of this horror show was I at least had the good luck to crash within the vicinity of Kootenai Medical Center, with some of the best medical professionals in the country. And that was a damn good thing, because I was apparently quite a handful. I pulled out my own PIC line in the middle of the night, and they had to call Laura and wake her up to get her permission to surgically implant it in my upper arm so I couldn't pull it out again.

Despite being monitored 24/7, I kept trying to get out of bed after being transferred to the neuro-ortho unit a few days later. My leg was heavily bandaged, and I was attached to a continuous passive movement machine that slowly bent and unbent my knee to keep it from locking up. I somehow managed to lift the entire contraption over the guardrail of the bed. Fortunately, my daughter Tristen and my son Josh were there to catch me. Just as the weight of the machine was carrying me over the side of the bed, they dove to save me—likely preventing yet another TBI, since I certainly would have hit my head on the hard hospital floor. It took them and two nurses to get me and the apparatus safely back into bed. When I was able to get up and around, I had to use a walker and keep my right leg bent upward behind me since I was required to be "non-weight bearing" for three months. Of course, my memory was shot, so I'd forget and try to walk to the bathroom without a walker, or I'd forget to keep my leg up. So, they tied me to my chair. The new Greg was on lockdown. Little did they know I was in my euphoric safe place.

In addition to being a danger to myself, I was also a pain in the ass—though, the technical term is "disinhibited." First there was the lying. Tristen says that when the nurses asked how I was doing, I'd say, "Pretty dang good!" They'd ask me what my pain levels were, on a scale of one to ten, and I'd say, "Two point nine." When the nurse left, my kids would ask, "Dad, what's your pain level really at?" I would answer, "Seven-point-one. And it would be a little slice of heaven if you'd go out to my Harley and get me some Advil so I could get the hell out of here!"

Of course, the kind of pain meds I was on would have made Advil look like candy and would have been the worst medicine for a brain bleed. The medical team had to keep the pain meds relatively low in order to track my coma rating and neurological reactions. I moaned in pain and moved restlessly in bed, but if I'd been completely drugged up, they wouldn't have been able to monitor my recovery. So, apparently, the pain continued, and I badgered everyone in sight for Advil: Laura, Jimmy, family, doctors, nurses, janitors, food delivery folks, nursing assistants, techs, clergy, social workers, therapists, and the highway patrolmen from the crash site who continued to visit us. Prior to my accident, Advil was my over-the-counter med of choice for curing all my stress headaches and hangovers. I took it with me on all my rides and adventures. Now? Not one pill. Son of a bitch! But, this was all physical. Internally it didn't matter. In my safe place and had no pain. None.

And then there was the rude, stubborn behavior. Laura says I *hated* the food at Kootenai. Hated it. Much to my family's embarrassment, I would loudly and frequently refer to the food as "dog shit" that "wasn't meant to be consumed by humans." I asked Laura and Debbie to flush it down the toilet and tell the nurses I'd eaten it. Mind you, the whole reason I was in this mess in the first place was because I ate that funky trout. And now I'm suddenly a snob? I used to eat sardines with my dad. Who was this new guy? Plus, in reality, the food at Kootenai was so good, family members would finish the meals I turned my nose up at. I even turned away a chocolate milkshake, which was basically my favorite food group. Knowing that, Debbie brought me one hoping I would eat something. After taking two sips, I said it tasted like crap. My refusal to eat was a big problem. From a neurological standpoint, the Kootenai team knew I'd have a better chance of reaching higher levels of recovery if my stomach was getting as much attention as my brain.

I was stubborn too—fending off much-needed help, like when Laura tried to help me shower and use my walker. I would obstinately (and incorrectly) insist to her that I could do things on own. "I can do this myself. You don't have to help me take a shower! I've been doing this my whole life!" She saved my life and now I was being an ass? To Laura? Who was I? That wasn't Greg.

Throughout my ten-day stay at Kootenai, when I was awake, my behavior was all over the place. I was letting it *all* hang out—including, but not limited to, my butt from my hospital gown. "I don't like this place," I'd say. "Get me the hell out of here." When I pulled out my catheter, the nurses joked that I'd better behave, or they'd put it back in. Seriously! The pain of pulling out my catheter was probably close to lethal, but I was jacked up. My synapses weren't firing on "all eight." Still, it's a mystery to me—why didn't my behavior match the blissful peacefulness I was feeling? Why the outer rebellion if I was feeling such inner peace?

But it wasn't all bad. Sometimes I managed to make people laugh. One night, it was after nine o'clock and the ICU was dark. Debbie and Laura were in my room sitting by my bedside. A guitarist was playing a sweet melody for another patient down the hall. I was comatose and Debbie was comforting Laura. Out of nowhere I began to sing, "When I Go Down to the River to Pray" from the movie *Oh Brother Where Art Thou*, one of my favorites. I've always been a huge music lover. I sang it twice, softly, with my eyes closed, without waking from my coma—like I was singing in my sleep. Laura said this couldn't have come at a better time; she was desperately in need of some levity. She and my sister couldn't believe what had just happened. They tried to get me to sing it again, but nothing. I was out. They just giggled together. That was so me.

Another humorous moment occurred thanks to Debbie and a Sweet'N Low packet. Debbie thinks I'm sweet all the time. She only has sweet thoughts about me, even when I'm not deserving of them. She's always been my protector and has overlooked my faults. Of course, I didn't know it at the time, but Laura told me later that Debbie stuck a Sweet'N Low packet underneath a little hook above the bedpost right above my head. It's very endearing to me. Just one of those little things that brought a little comfort and sweetness to a dark time.

With TBI, there's no telling what kind of personality changes a person may undergo—and which of those changes will be permanent. Many survivors experience personality changes depending on where in their brain the injuries are located. Sometimes these changes impact a person's relationships and level of recovery. Therapists were telling Laura that the changes she was seeing in me might be a preview of the Greg she'd get as I aged. Quite honestly, it takes time for personalities to solidify after a TBI, and all kinds of input determine what sticks—support networks, getting the right tools from neuro rehab, a person's own work ethic and problem-solving capacity, exercise, good nutrition, plenty of sleep, giving back, gratitude, and so on.

Wherever I would land, it was yet to be determined. The way I was acting was a million miles out of character for me. Now, mind you, I don't remember a thing from this entire time at Kootenai. Even though I was interacting with folks, I wasn't really "there." I spoke in a flat, unemotional tone and said things that were nonsensical or impulsive. Laura was watching my behavior and constantly wondering "Is *this* the guy?" Was she forever to be saddled with this version of me? Dr. Bowen, who went out of his way to visit often and talk with Laura, tried to reassure her that my strange behavior wouldn't last forever, but still, she was understandably worried about the prospect.

10

The moments when I was awake, all I wanted to do was go home. I had it in my head that all I needed to do was pop some meds and I'd be good to go. I could comprehend very little of what I was experiencing and couldn't remember much from day to day or even from one hour to the next. I felt like I was being left out of the loop, and I began to get paranoid that the medical team wasn't being truthful with me. I argued with Dr. Ganz, telling him that I should be able to go home. I asked to see the CT scans for myself, but of course I wouldn't have even been able to understand what I was looking at.

Finally, after much pushing—and I'm sure Laura had a huge sway over the decision—Dr. Ganz gave us permission to check out on August 24, ten days after I'd been admitted, to be transferred to Intermountain Medical Center (IMC) in Salt Lake City, Utah. So, not quite the "home" I'd been asking for, but close enough. Back to Salt Lake where all my friends and family were.

Coordinating the transfer from Coeur d'Alene to Salt Lake was a tremendous undertaking. My good friend LeeAnne, who was an executive vice president at the bank I worked for, helped Laura and our counselors coordinate the transfer with IMC's staff. LeeAnne was also on the board of the Urban District of Intermountain Healthcare, which helped immensely with the transfer. Jimmy, was able to borrow a 206 Cessna from the corporation he flew for, thanks to the owner's generosity, which saved us the big expense of chartering a medical flight. Laura had to ship our luggage, since there wouldn't be enough room for it on the plane. And those were just the logistics—there was also my condition to worry about. Dr. Ganz examined me early that morning to make sure I could handle the flight, and the medical team stockpiled us with ample medication and helped Laura get me ready. By this time, Laura and Dr. Ganz had grown close. She has a special talent for digging through a person's outer layers, and she'd gotten to know him on a personal level. So, though they'd met under stressful circumstances, they parted as friends by the time we checked out of Kootenai.

My occupational therapist at Kootenai was a man named Bill who'd lost an arm in a motorcycle accident years earlier. While I was generally well-behaved during my sessions with him, he saw the ways that I was obstinate with Laura. So, in preparation for the flight, he pulled Laura aside and said that if I misbehaved, she would need to put on her "harsh face," yell at me sternly and take action. The biggest risk during flight was for me to lose control and attempt to open the plane's door and get out. Laura was ready for anything, and she had the meds if needed.

Fortunately, the flight went smoothly—I slept through it and hardly made a peep. It's odd to think I spent probably the most crucial ten days of my life in Coeur d'Alene and don't remember a single thing about it. I see photos, like a picture of myself in the airplane, decked out in sunglasses and totally conked out. But I have no memories of the events or of the amazing medical team and first responders who saved my life.

After landing in Utah, my son-in-law Brant picked us up from the hanger, drove us to Intermountain Medical Center, and we checked in to the Neuro Specialty Rehabilitation Center, room 1219. Within seconds of getting into my new bed, I was asleep, but my new medical team went to work right away. Dr. Dodds, a neuro rehabilitation specialist, and Dr. Ryser, director of the rehab group, met with Laura and assured her that the team was ready for me. Susan, one of my new neuro rehab RNs, did an initial assessment—and of course, put alarms on my bed and assigned me 24/7 coverage, since my reputation as a "flight risk" had preceded me.

That night, I was surrounded by family, and once again experienced the incredible euphoria of a deep, internal connection with them. I was able to connect with some of my family members—like Jodi and Jeremy—who hadn't been able to meet us in Coeur d'Alene. I only remember bits of strange events about that first day. The events themselves are blurry. But the internal connections I felt were vivid. I could feel their warm touch and hear their familiar voices. There's a misconception about coma—a lot of people think we can't hear or recognize when our loved ones are in our midst. But that's not true, or at least it wasn't true for me. I distinctly remember the feeling of being in a safe space, surrounded by love and protected from all else. The love of my family was healing to me.

11

I woke suddenly in a complete state of confusion. I was standing upright, holding onto some sort of mechanical device with wheels, stumbling along on one leg. I didn't even have a context for what a "walker" was, let alone the word for it. Behind me stood a strange man, and he seemed to be directing me to hop toward a doorway within a hospital room. *What the hell? What was happening?*

I immediately began to panic. I couldn't see anything familiar and something was seriously wrong inside of me. Where was Laura? That question dominated my focus. I looked everywhere around that sterile room, but all I could see was the bed, a bright window and florescent lights that made my brain scream out in anxiety. The smells of chlorine and harsh detergent were being injected into my nose. Where was Laura? I let go of the "walker" and swung my left arm in a wide arc, forcing the stranger out from behind me. There she was. Laura with her sweet smile appeared and our eyes met. Without saying a word, I felt in an instant that all was good.

At the same moment, I knew the stranger behind me was a nurse, and I knew why he was directing me to the other room. We were heading toward the bathroom, because I needed to get to a toilet, *now*! I didn't know it, but I'd just been given an enema—and it had woken me up from a coma. For real this time. How's that for a medical miracle? Fortunately, the next miracle was that I made it to the bathroom in time. Whew.

And that is how, after a week and a half of protection in my safe state of bliss, I was booted unceremoniously back into reality. I was filled suddenly with all of the fear and confusion I'd been protected from when I was in my place of contentment. The real physical world—and the real physical reality—was all back, kind of.

The odd thing, everybody else was under the impression that I'd been awake the whole time. I'd been acting weird as hell, sure, and much of what I was saying didn't make any sense—I was forgetting words and substituting them with words and phrases from banking. But I'd been engaging in conversation and seemed to be awake, and there were even moments when I appeared to be lucid. I'd been participating in rehab therapies. But I have no memory of anything before the enema. My body was there, but my experience was in my safe place. I had a sense of being internally connected with Josh, Tristen, Debbie, and Laura in Idaho. Whenever one of them would enter the room, I felt a lightning bolt of loving energy. I knew when they were there. They held my hands and spoke to me, and I felt their love, courage, and hope. Each one of them had their own signature, each so strong that it felt tangible, like something I could grasp and hold on to. It was carrying me.

What they could see was me misbehaving, and not being myself. But I wasn't really there. My own sense of awareness and of myself was that I was in a safe and loving, euphoric realm with no time and no pain. Peace in its purest form. I look at pictures of myself from that time, and I think, "That is not me." One photo shows me sitting on the edge of a hospital bed, looking down at the floor and staring blankly, while a speech therapist touches my shoulder. Another photo shows a man shaving my face as I stare blankly ahead. I wasn't really there.

And now, abruptly, I was "back" for real. I didn't question it—at all. I also didn't question going back and forth between my coma and reality, either. It all seemed normal and blissful to me. Hell, what did I know? All I knew was I felt blissful and full of warmth and love in both realms. Waking up was happiness at its depth. It was wonderment to lock eyes with my partner physically. An extension of our internal connection in my tranquil sea of love.

Once Laura helped the nurse get me to the bathroom and then back into bed, I was filled with questions. *Where was I? What happened?* Of course, these were the questions I'd asked a million times in Idaho, but I couldn't remember the answers. When Laura—who was exasperated by having to repeat herself yet again—told me the basics of my situation, I was floored. Wow. It hit me that I'd had several days' worth of physical experiences and conversations in Idaho that I had no memory of.

In my mind, this was the moment I actually woke up from the coma. This was the moment I returned to myself. I still don't remember much of that first day. I know we had some sort of family gathering and I had my first speech therapy session. But I was zoning in and out, fuzzy and fatigued, and I have only glimpses of those events in my memory. That's how I would describe the entire first month of coming awake: little bits of memory, just glimpses here and there. And the more time went by, the glimpses of memory extended—the short little bits became connected and grew into longer bits, which created a more coherent picture of my situation.

Sometimes a coma is not about waking up just once. There were many moments of awakening. Pieces came together and gelled in my mind, and when they gelled, they became awareness—and I became aware that I was in deep shit.

12

I don't know what all that enema knocked loose, but from the instant I woke up, I was changed. Gone was pain-in-the-ass, unpredictable Greg. In his place was a star student who wanted nothing more than to work hard and be praised. My memory came back gradually, but the shift in my attitude was instantaneous. Whereas before I was sometimes obstinate or unwilling to follow orders, now all I wanted was to please people. How's that for a plot twist?

That first day at IMC, they started me on speech therapy. One of the activities was to engage the patient in "free conversation." Basically, they just get you talking. My therapist Kamie asked, "Tell me what happened to bring you here?" and here's how I answered: "*I just shirt. Claustrophobic—kind of. Three days. Well actually longer than that. Pasted a lot first go. And then I tried to share regarding claustrophobia. So it just happened.*" She had no idea what I was trying to say, and neither do I. Clearly, I had a long way to go. Also, I'm pretty sure that, given I'd just been treated to an enema, Kamie probably added the "r" into "shirt." That was tactful of her.

As I gradually got my wits about me, I started to figure out what I could and couldn't do. My short-term memory was getting better, but there was a significant downside to this: I was starting to remember from day to day what was wrong with me. I had moments of awareness, that actually awakened me to all of the things I could no longer do; pretty important things like speaking, reading, writing, and comprehending. Damn, looking back, I can't believe it didn't totally freak me out. I also had to relearn other basic tasks like grooming and hygiene. And I had to do this all while literally standing on one leg—I wouldn't be able to put weight on my damaged leg for weeks. Talk about a circus act.

Fortunately, when I came out of the coma, I was ready to work hard. I had the mindset of a young boy. I was relearning basic human skills, and so my behavior and demeanor became boyish as well. All I wanted to do was please the "adults" around me and hear their words of praise. I was reliving my childhood. As a kid, I wanted to do everything well. I wanted to do well in class, have friends, be active, and excel.

One of my earliest childhood memories is of watching my parents and sisters have a blow-out battle with my older brother, who passed away nine months before my accident. As a teenager, my brother was completely out-of-hand at times, and fights with him would involve doors torn off hinges and lots of screaming—especially with two of my strongest sisters. Their battles were epic and vicious sometimes. After one skirmish, my parents were sobbing in their bedroom. I told them I would never behave like that. My sister Debbie was the closest to my age and she protected me during the battles. She would distract me and say, "Greg-o" let's play games in the closet for a while." She would find a place for us to hide.

I loved to hear my parents say they were proud of me and that I was doing a good job as a young boy. I was extremely driven to please my parents and perform well in school, sports, playing the drums, and getting along with my family. Praise from my parents was everything growing up. That desire to do good and be good reasserted itself in a huge way when I came out of the coma.

So, I was highly motivated—and that was a good thing, because I had a *lot* of work ahead of me. I was experiencing severe posttraumatic amnesia, aphasia, and semantic paraphasia. During posttraumatic amnesia, new events can't be stored in the memory, and can't be regained, because they're not encoded properly. As I healed, islands of memory would form, separated by oceans of emptiness. Gradually, the islands became bigger and bigger, and merged together into a cohesive landscape, and I could track and remember events and conversations. But it took a while to fully return to reality. It was a hazy, disorienting time—to put it mildly—and was compounded, of course, by my other problems with aphasia and semantic paraphasia.

Aphasia is an umbrella term for a range of language impairments, and can include difficulty remembering words or being unable to speak, read, write, or comprehend language. Aphasia is experienced differently, of course, based on which area of the brain is damaged and to what extent. My neuro team told us that my aphasia was primarily a "motor expressive" type, which resulted in damaged articulation; I struggled to get words out, and I stuttered. At times, I also exhibited "receptive aphasia," which meant I had difficulty understanding the spoken word, even when I myself was speaking somewhat normally. Reading, speaking, writing, and comprehension were all extremely difficult.

Semantic paraphasia can cause substitution errors or speaking in word fragments—sometimes without even knowing you're doing it. For me, I often inserted banking terms into my speech, like asking one of my sons, Jer, "How is your loan presentation going?" and "What loan presentations are you doing tomorrow?" What I *thought* I was asking him was, "How is your first semester at the

University of Utah going?" and "What classes are you going to tomorrow?" Sometimes strange or nonsensical phrases would come out of my mouth, or I couldn't speak at all.

Aphasia made it hard to remember names and faces, and for me to understand and verbalize what I was seeing. After hobbling back to my room on my walker after one of my occupational therapy sessions with Lesha, my daughter Jodi was there with her kids Brody and Laney. I was thrilled to see them—until Lesha tested me by asking who they were. Late afternoons and evenings can be the hardest part of the day for TBI survivors. Fatigue sets in hard, and for me this is when my aphasia issues peak and I have the most difficult time with cognitive function and speaking. When I was spent at the end of the day, I was screwed if someone cornered me. That day, I was exhausted after several therapy sessions and physician visits. I panicked and couldn't remember their names. Can you imagine not being able to remember the names of your own kids and grandkids? I felt horrible instantly and didn't want them to feel bad. I didn't want to look stupid either. But then, I focused on Laney and seemingly out of nowhere I remembered the history of her name. Neuroplasticity was working, helping my brain to remap itself, while I was in "fight or flight" mode, pumping adrenaline into my synapses. I blurted out, "Lesha, this is Wayne. Her name is Laney but we call her 'Waney' or 'Wayne.'" Whew. I never knew when my mind would serve up in a given moment, but I got lucky that time. To this day, Jodi tells that story fondly.

Initially, I didn't realize I had aphasia issues and I got frustrated when people didn't understand me. One of my family members, after visiting and witnessing me firsthand, looked over at Laura, eyebrows raised, and said, "Greg's in trouble." Early on, my problems were so steep I didn't even know I had problems. Over time, I started to comprehend that these speaking impairments were real problems and I'd have to focus earnestly in order to rehab successfully. In her notes from that first week, Kamie wrote that I told her, "I have difficulty understanding people's language." Another speech pathologist, Margaret, indicated I was stressed and wrote in her charting notes that I said, "I'm worried to get my brain right." Though, for whatever reason, I didn't become anxious or overwhelmed or focus on what I couldn't do. I was patient with myself. I was excited to do what was asked of me, especially initially, when I thought I was just pleasing those around me. Dr. Dodds made daily rounds in the morning, and I always tried to wake up quickly when he arrived. I wanted him to know I was diligently working to do more than he and the therapists asked of me. I bonded with Dr. Dodds on the twelfth floor as he acknowledged my hard work. He saw the small stuff, like working on my therapy modules in my room, and he would say, "Greg, you're doing your homework." That would make me laugh. I hoped he would see my efforts and be happy with me.

I did the same with everyone on the medical team—neurologists, surgeons, psychologists, therapists, and nurses. My CNA, Karen, made an extra effort to become my friend. She was a hugger. Her healing warmth would envelope me. She would say between therapy sessions, "Greg you need to eat your lunch, buddy." She knew I didn't like food, but I would eat when Karen asked me to. I loved having someone ask me to do a task. They were really simple activities like repeating phrases, playing games, naming cards, making muffins out of a box, putting dishes away, or stretching out my leg. But I was like a young boy in rehab, and these tasks were extremely hard. I would work diligently and then wait for their response. All they had to say was, "Greg, you're doing great!" and I was instantly elevated. It was surreal. I didn't know it at the time, but my desire to please helped me push myself and work harder than I might have otherwise, and I was improving ahead of expectations.

In my second speech therapy session with Kamie that first week at IMC, she had me put together simple wooden puzzles covered with pictures of animals, and then asked me to name the animals. This is a moment I'll never forget. The four-piece puzzle took me twenty minutes to figure out, and when it was done I found myself looking at a picture of a butterfly. I knew what it was, but I couldn't get the word out of my mouth. The aphasia made it hard for me to understand and verbalize what I was seeing. It was heart wrenching and I started to cry tears of frustration and sadness.

After Kamie helped calm me down, she had me tell her about my daily routines. When I told her I was used to reading the *Wall Street Journal* on my computer each morning, she asked me to show her. I had no idea that Laura was behind me, watching all of this go down, but she says I reached right over to Kamie's computer and typed in "wsj.com" out of habit. They were both flabbergasted and couldn't believe I'd just accessed a website in the midst of having severe aphasia problems. I couldn't remember the word "butterfly" for crying out loud, but I could pull up the *Journal* on the internet.

This was a lightbulb moment for Laura. Watching me use Kamie's computer immediately gave her an idea. As soon as the speech pathology session was over, she drove straight to the Apple store. She told the nearest sales person that she wanted their best iPad and didn't care how much it cost. It was an emotional purchase for Laura, and she had intense hope that it would help me get my brain back to normal. That night, she brought the new iPad to room 1219 and handed it to me in bed. I'd wanted an iPad for a long time, so Laura and I were both excited. She showed me all the iPad apps and helped me work on it daily. Over time, I learned how to download brain-training apps, which were tremendous to my cognitive rehab. Most of them were puzzles and games that challenged my memory and my mental flexibility and speed. Some of the apps were for kids, which was okay by me. I would play them constantly on my iPad and in my speech therapy sessions. I didn't know at the time that I was remapping my brain and relearning basic human skills. All I knew was that I had a cool Apple product in my hands and I was having a blast. Rockin'!

Kamie was always tender with me and tried to help me understand I was dealing with aphasia issues. I remember her saying the word "aphasia," but I couldn't comprehend its meaning. Margaret, who also helped me in speech pathology, wrote in her notes that I said, "I can't figure all this out." That one simple sentence summed up my internal mindset during neuro rehab. Looking back years later, from the vantage point of having made an incredible recovery, it's easy to connect the dots and see how I was able to regain my abilities with the help of a highly skilled medical team, supportive family, and my intrinsic motivation to work my butt off. But at the time, we had no idea what lay ahead. My family and friends were caring and calm in my presence, despite having to answer all my repetitive questions, but they probably had anxiety when they were away from me—especially Laura. I was morphing daily, and with each new change Laura was asking herself, "Is *this* the guy? Is this who Greg is going to be from now on?"

13

I was having a hard time formulating questions in my mind and getting the right words out, and much of the time I couldn't fully comprehend or remember what others were saying. I was often fatigued, my head ached, and I got overwhelmed easily by bright lights and loud noises. I couldn't handle having too many people in my room. But still, I doggedly returned to my questions—"obsessed" is the word Jimmy used to describe me. I *had* to know what had happened to me. I started getting worried about my job. I obsessed about going back to work. About paying bills.

My need to feel informed was complicated by the fact that my memory was shot. My rehab team would, of course, answer all of my many questions, but I would quickly forget the details and then later I'd wonder why they hadn't talked to me. I realized finally that I was being monitored continuously, and that I was being watched and had to get permission to do what I wanted. This got me paranoid. Laura assured me that everyone was being open and honest, but I still felt like something secretive was happening.

One night after Laura left to go home, a nurse's aide sat next to me, in what I'd come to think of as "Laura's chair." He pulled her chair up close to my bed. I got frustrated and territorial about Laura's chair. I couldn't sleep and didn't know what to do about it. Finally, I asked him to leave, but he explained that it was his job to take care of me. I got emotional and began to tear up, so he moved to just outside my door where he could still keep an eye on me. Finally, I fell asleep.

In the morning, I asked a nurse if I could call Laura. This was a first. I hadn't even thought to make a phone call before this and didn't realize there wasn't even a phone in my room. Laura had put the room's phone in a drawer, as I learned later, because she didn't want me having access to it during those early days. She was concerned about my inability to have a coherent conversation and wanted to prevent me from being in a position where I might say something that I would regret later, especially to the executives of the bank I worked for. So, they brought the phone out. Laura's name and phone number were written on the white board on the wall near my bed. A nurse dialed, and Laura answered. I got emotional and cried while telling her what had happened the night before. I didn't want anyone sitting in her chair or watching me in secret.

Laura was able to calm me, and to reassure me (probably not for the first time...) that the medical staff were great, and they were doing their job really well. Laura said I could call her anytime. What? I could make a decision on my own? I could decide to make a call to someone, on a phone, at any time? This was a huge awakening moment. From that day on, I called Laura every morning when I woke up—and no one sat in her chair again without my permission. Of course, these probably don't seem like big deals, but to me these small measures of control were lifelines at a time when I had very little agency.

This whole time, I'd been telling anyone in earshot that I wanted to go home. Kamie said I asked if I could be "released" from rehab after a speech pathology session in my first week. I had an idea that if I could just go home, life would return to normal. In fact, I was so focused on going home, I didn't want to let anything stand in my way—including the broken hand I'd been hiding. My physical therapist, who was also named Laura, had me try walking with crutches. The pressure on my right hand was incredibly painful, but I didn't want to tell anyone because I thought it meant they wouldn't let me go home.

Laura, my wife, saw that my hand was puffy. She realized it was a serious problem once it became obvious to her that going up and down the stairs and walking the lap around the twelfth floor was intensely painful for me, despite my attempts to hide it. She told Dr. Dodds, and he had an orthopedic surgeon take a look. But after taking an x-ray, the IMC surgeon confirmed it was broken. The bone below my middle finger, in my palm, was broken diagonally in half. Since it had been more than two weeks since the accident, the bones were beginning to knit already. Swelling was minimal, and it didn't hurt unless I put pressure on it—like trying to use crutches or lift something heavy. Dr. Dodds and the surgeon recommended immediate surgery to break apart the beginning of the fusion. They'd re-break the bones of my "flipping the bird" finger, set it properly, and cast my hand until it healed.

Well, as you can imagine, when I heard that plan, I went berserk. All I could think was, "Oh, hell no! You're not putting me back into surgery and making me stay longer in the hospital, dammit!" After the mini fit, they came up with an alternate plan. Rather than putting me through more surgery, they splinted the hand, which was fine by me. Lesha handmade a splint out of molded plastic, which was pretty dang cool to be a part of. After about the tenth attempt at hot molding (which entailed warming two pieces of medical plastic and then using her hands and a steel tool to shape them to fit the top and bottom of my hand), she got the splint perfectly sized to my right hand. Then she attached some Velcro straps and a University of Utah logo since, as you should know, I'm a "Ute" fan, and surgery was avoided. To me, surgery would have just meant more delay standing between me and the sweet relief of going home. Laura (physical therapist) added braces to my walker and crutches to help take pressure off the hand so it could heal up.

Ten days after I'd been transferred to IMC, I heard about a magical thing called a "half-day pass," which would allow me to leave the confines of the hospital for a few hours. And boy did I want it. I pestered my wife and my medical team until they agreed to help prep me for an adventure. They asked me what kind of activity I'd like to do—go to the movies, or the mall—but all I wanted to do was sit on the back deck of my home with Laura. That was my happy place. I wanted to sit on the deck with a cup of coffee and a copy of the *Salt Lake Tribune*.

Lesha helped me practice getting from the twelfth floor, into the elevator, and down to the car with my wheelchair and walker, and to get into the car safely without putting any weight on my leg. Once the team was confident I could navigate that, they gave me the half-day pass. My dream was finally coming true.

At home, sitting in my wheelchair on our deck, I felt the glow of the sun warming my body. It was early September and fall was in the air. It's my favorite time of year. Not too hot and definitely no snow yet. Holding the *Salt Lake Tribune* in my hands, caressing its thin, gritty paper, knowing black ink would be smeared on each of my fingerprints, was heaven. How could this glorious moment in time be anything but blissful? But... then I looked down. No! Looking at the front page, all I saw was a garbled mess of letters. I couldn't read a word. I couldn't even comprehend the structure of the paper. Columns, headlines, pictures with scrambled letters underneath, and more stuff on the side. I didn't get it. WTF!? I didn't tell Laura. I couldn't. I couldn't admit to her or myself at the time. But deep down, I knew. This was one of my biggest moments of awareness and awakening. I couldn't read.

While the half-day passes were great gifts, they also gave me a taste of the freedom I longed for. From the window of my room on the twelfth floor, I could see downtown Salt Lake City. I knew I lived right across from the state capitol building, over Memory Grove, next to LDS Hospital. I didn't have all my wits about me, but I knew landmarks. And I just wanted to go home.

Everyone tried to stall me when I pushed to get out. I simply didn't understand the ramifications of going home too early, and I really didn't comprehend what it would be like for Laura. I'd ask, "When can I go? When can I go?" and the person would either not answer, or they'd put me off with something vague like "Maybe in a few days." In hindsight, I can now see why they all wanted me to stay. I could have used a bit more healing time in hospital. Of course, I didn't think I needed to be in the hospital—I thought I was a rock star and I wanted everything yesterday—but I was obviously not in a position to make that assessment. I've always thought I could handle more than I really could. Three traumatic brain injuries pretty much sums it up.

You can never go backward, and it's pretty tough to tell a patient anything, especially someone as pigheaded as me. I probably wouldn't have listened or taken no for an answer. And so, I pushed and pushed to go home, and finally wore everyone down. Physically, I was on the mend. My leg was healing well. One of my nurses, my sweet RN Julie who went out of her way to become a good friend to us, took out the staples that held together the incisions on my right knee and shin, as well as the stitches from out of my big toenail. Without all of the hardware and wrappings, my leg looked huge and weirdly shaped from the swelling and scarring. My toe looked positively alien. As for my brain, Laura told me later that Dr. Dodds showed us a new CT scan which showed all the blood on my brain had dissipated, and there was no more hemorrhaging or bruising. The right side had shrunk a little, but that's normal for brain injury survivors. In her notes from that day, Laura quipped, "The Advil ban has been lifted. Praise be to God. Idaho people will appreciate that."

Lesha came home with us one last time to check out the house and make sure I could navigate it safely. I showed her how I could scoot up and down the stairs on my butt, using my left hand and left leg for leverage while keeping my right leg elevated. Lesha gave Laura some instructions as far as keeping rugs and furniture safely out of my path. My sons Josh and Jeremy, and my daughter-in-law Amanda, helped Laura move the furniture in our bedroom to accommodate my walker. (They got a good laugh about all the snacks they found next to my side of the bed.) My sister Debbie let us borrow a shower chair. It seemed like whatever we needed, there was someone to pitch in. Home was ready for me, and I was definitely ready for it.

Nurse Julie talked to us about how life would be after my release from the hospital. She shared her warmth with us and chatted with Laura about her life in Park City. They became true friends, which Laura needed. It helped take Laura's mind off the losses she was experiencing. Julie knew the burden Laura was about to face, and was preparing her as best as she could. Julie and the neuro rehab team worked all hours for me and cared for Laura.

And so, finally, on September 9, 2011, almost a month after my accident, I checked out of the hospital. Janet, my discharge RN, wheeled me out of room 1219 and down the elevator. She hugged me and helped load me into Laura's red sport Mini Clubman. Wheelchair and walker were crammed into the back through the split-wide rear doors. But if I had known what I was about to put Laura through, I wouldn't have let Janet put me in the Mini.

14

Pulling out of IMC's hospital complex for the final time is a vague memory and almost feels like another lifetime. The drive home was surreal. Even though I desperately wanted to be home in our sanctuary, I'd become grounded to my hospital routines and didn't completely trust my ability to be away from my familiar room 1219. I held on to Laura during the ride to make sure it was legitimate. We drove downtown on I-15, which is one of my most frequently traveled routes. It's carved in my memory. Taking it from the passenger seat, watching billboards fly by with half my brain functioning, was new. My sense of self was changing daily, my old self becoming more distant.

After the hell and anguish of the previous month, it was a relief to go home and do simple things I had taken for granted, like being able to sleep beside Laura in bed or sit on my living room couch, which immediately became my rehab "command center" for the next few months. But what I didn't realize then is that, in my eagerness to get out of the hospital, I had put Laura in the role of full-time caretaker. She was making a huge personal sacrifice for me. Our insurance didn't cover any at-home healthcare support, and initially, I had to have someone around me at all times. Whereas at the hospital we had a whole team of experts on hand, at home the lion's share of the burden fell to Laura. She was nervous about having to take on responsibilities that felt like they were over her head. Later, she admitted that she would have felt better if I'd stayed in the hospital just a little longer, since she felt more secure having everything and everyone we needed right there. But at the time, she didn't feel like she could say that, especially since I was so clearly anxious to get home. She didn't want to seem unsupportive.

I didn't know any of this; at the time, I unknowingly overestimated my abilities, was "very casual with safety" (as one of my physical therapists put it), and I still had on the proverbial rose-colored lenses of my bliss state, which buffered my awareness of the severity and stress of my situation. I truly had no idea what I'd asked Laura to take on. The way I'd pictured it, I'd hobble into the house and life would get itself back on track. But, of course, that wasn't the case. Our daily life changed dramatically. It was incredibly difficult for Laura to see me, back in our familiar home but so changed, and so unable to participate in the life that we'd built together. She was suffering a great deal with the sudden upheaval, but really had no time to process her own grief. My rehab gave me purpose, at least temporarily, but it left Laura with a hole in her life—and extreme worry about our future.

And, the cherry on top? Once I got home, I couldn't stop telling Laura how much I missed all the staff at the hospital and how much I loved it there. "I miss my room! I miss so-and-so!" This went on for a while until Laura finally quipped, "Well, if you miss them so much, why don't you go back?" She was half kidding, of course. She could understand that I'd gotten attached to the people who'd done so much for me during a critical time in my life. But still, there was an odd dynamic. As Laura describes it, I seemed to have a distorted view of how long I'd been in the hospital. I kept saying things like "Since I got home..." as if I'd been gone for months or years as opposed to weeks. I spoke as if I'd been away overseas for a year, or had gone to prison, or had lived in an ashram in India. Some place far removed from my day-to-day reality.

15

During my first week back at home, I sat at a stool at our kitchen island, eating a bowl of Frosted Flakes, which had become my new favorite cereal. I'd never been much of a breakfast person after my childhood, but Dr. Dodds wanted me to continue my newly established routines, and eating three times a day was one of them. Even though they were more so thinking of balanced meals with lots of proteins, fruits, and veggies, they were just glad I was willing to eat something in the morning.

I lost twenty-five pounds while I was in the hospital because my taste and sense of smell had changed and foods I normally loved just didn't taste good to me anymore. But while I was there I'd developed a fondness for Frosted Flakes again. I used to love them when I was a kid. Tony the Tiger was a cool dude. While I was eating at the kitchen island, I was telling Laura that I wished I could be more helpful around the house. Normally I was in charge of doing dishes and setting the coffee machine at night. I missed being useful. Laura came up behind me, wrapped her arms around me, and assured me I'd soon be able to help again.

Just then, seemingly out of nowhere, I began to feel unwell. Laura watched as my right hand started to tremble as I held the spoon, and I began to slur my words and mumble. I passed out, right there at the island. Fortunately, Laura still had her arms around me and was able to hold on to me from the back to keep me from falling off the chair and onto the tile floor. She grasped me tightly for a few minutes until I came to. I was shaking, and it took me a moment to realize what had just happened. Tears came to my eyes, and I felt lightheaded and sick to my stomach. Laura didn't know what to do—she didn't want to let go of me. When I calmed down, she was able to help me to the couch before frantically calling Dr. Dodds. He said to get me to the emergency room, now. The hospital was only a block away.

We made it to the front of the hospital before I started to throw up. I should have opened the car window, but I didn't have my wits about me. I was covered in cereal.

Dr. Dodds had called the ER team to let them know I was on my way, and they were waiting for us outside (gloves on, hands up—again...). When Laura told them I'd just eaten Frosted Flakes, they said, "We wish you hadn't told us. We like to guess!" That made Laura laugh even though we were stressed. Personally, I was embarrassed. What a waste of Flakes.

Suspecting I may have had a seizure, the ER team treated me to yet another CT scan and a round of tests. But, after a few hours, with ER docs consulting with Dr. Dodds, a seizure was ruled out. They released me, and Laura and I went away that day without an answer.

However, within the next month, it happened twice more. I came down with the flu and passed out once in the bathroom and once in the bedroom, each time just as scary and nerve-wracking. Thankfully, Laura was there with me both times and was able to catch me before I went down like a bag of rocks.

After this, Dr. Dodds gave me a diagnosis that put my entire situation into a new light: vasovagal syncope. This is caused when there's a disruption to the vagus nerve, which connects your brain stem to your intestinal tract. When it gets interrupted—which can be caused by stress or illness, like food poisoning or the flu—it can cause a significant decrease in blood pressure, which can lead to fainting. Dr. Dodds said this is most likely what caused my Harley accident after I got food poisoning from that funky fish.

This was an "ah-ah" moment for me and Laura. I'd always been a super-intense, anxious, type-A person, prone to driving myself to the limits. And when I'm stressed, my stomach gets upset. I'd had moments in the past where I'd passed out in tense situations or when I was ill, but I didn't know why and didn't investigate. I just shrugged it off as a weird oddity. When I recover from these episodes, I'm always completely out of it—I wake up not knowing where I am or what happened, and I'm foggy-headed, tearful, and wiped out physically and emotionally for most of the day. Of course, I don't remember how things went down during my crash, but I have a theory that I may have had the vasovagal syncope episode, passed out, and then regained consciousness mid-flight.

So, basically, the ultimate horror: waking up to find myself riding a Harley into a ditch. This would account for the bruises on my inner thighs and the broken hand; I may have woken up mid-accident and instantly heeded a gut instinct to stay on the bike. Fortunately, the benefit of having post-traumatic amnesia is that it clicked the terror-delete button on that gruesome memory.

16

As soon as I left the hospital, I started IMC's outpatient neuro rehab therapy in the basement of The Orthopedic Specialty Hospital (TOSH) three days a week, working on speech, occupational, and physical rehabilitation. Shortly after my release, I was in the TOSH rehab gym when I got the news that the orthopedic surgeon who'd taken care of me when I was an inpatient wasn't covered by my insurance now that I was outpatient.

At that point in my recovery, I was still fuzzy, and my problem-solving capabilities were next to nothing. When obstacles came at me, I couldn't fix them. Like when I was on the twelfth floor and couldn't figure out how to stop the nurses' aid from sitting in Laura's chair. I couldn't solve minor issues let alone great big ones like finding a new surgeon and dealing with the complexities of health insurance. And so, when I got the news that I'd need to find a new surgeon, I couldn't handle it. That seemed like way too high of a mountain to scale, and I just completely lost it and began bawling in the middle of the gym, with a bunch of therapists and patients staring at me.

A couple therapists came over to console me, and when they found out what I was so upset about, one of them said incredulously, "Greg, you're in the orthopedic specialty hospital of IMC. We've got great surgeons upstairs."

Yes, I was sitting in the orthopedic specialty unit and couldn't wrap my head around the process of getting a new orthopedic surgeon. Thinking back on it, that's funnier than hell. All of Intermountain Healthcare is under our insurance. We just had to walk one floor up and ask to speak to someone in the orthopedic wing. It was a quick phone call. "Of course!" They said. "Have him come up to see one of our knee specialists."

Unfortunately, that particular victory was short-lived, because the doctor we met with was a knee *replacement* specialist. He took one look at my x-rays and said, "This knee's gotta go." He wanted to give me a brand new one. But I'd just spent

67

what seemed like ages in the hospital, fixing and rehabbing my knee. I was waiting to start the process of becoming fully weight-bearing, and hoping to get approval from an orthopedic surgeon to do so. I'd already gone through so much to keep my own knee. Going through a major surgery to replace my own body part with a piece of titanium—that felt like a last resort. Your last resort as a human being.

I was completely confounded. Just getting in to see this guy had already taken a toll on me. Sitting in his patient room, I could have laid down and fallen asleep. I was completely fatigued. Totally wrung-out. So, I was already working with minimal mental resources, and, when the first thing out of his mouth after looking at that x-ray, was, "I want to replace your knee," I had zero capacity to handle that. I started sobbing. I'd just made it home after nearly a month in the hospital, and I was terrified at the thought of having to go back and have more surgery. I couldn't even say anything. I just looked at Laura and lost it. The surgeon tried talking to Laura, but she wasn't having it. She politely excused herself from his office and went into problem-solving mode—she went back out to the main desk and requested a different surgeon.

It was like night and day. The second surgeon, Dr. Trawick, specialized in traumatic knee injuries. He was kind, gentle, and warmhearted, and he sat us down and talked with us. He put me at ease immediately. He knew that I'd just come out of a coma and had been recommended by the neuro rehab team. I could sense from him that he could tell we'd just come through an unbelievable, tragic situation. It was a starkly different experience between these two surgeons' offices, and they were just a few doors away from each other. I felt like Dr. Trawick was in my corner. When he looked at new x-rays of my knee and foot, he was impressed with the work Dr. Bowen had done in Kootenai. I was glad to see that I hadn't screwed anything up with my haphazard attitude toward safety. Dr. Trawick talked me down from the cliff and reassured me that Dr. Bowen's skillful rebuild would hold together and I would walk, and even run again. Dr. Trawick gave me the go-ahead to start limited weight-bearing on my leg.

Now, if you were watching one of the *Rocky* movies right now, this would be where the training montage would begin. But instead of super-athlete Rocky Balboa, you'll have to picture me: a 49-year-old banker with a head injury and a walker, whose "breakfast of champions" is a bowl of Frosted Flakes (I'll leave the raw eggs to Rocky).

Being able to walk is awesome, and exercise is crucial to recovering cognitive functions and maintaining brain health throughout life. But the day-to-day physical therapy was a slog. The minutiae of it is hardly the stuff of a great story. It's just daunting work. I initially wrote a whole chapter about the various treatments I went through, because it seemed necessary to honor the hard work I did and to honor the professionals who helped me get there. But at the end of the day, it was just a daily grind.

Picture me sweating on a padded mat, getting my knee crunched, and then taking continuous rides on a stationary bike, supporting myself at the parallel bars to help add weight to my right leg, and finally lifting weights, until the physical therapist called it good. Rinse and repeat for months on end until gradually my strength and mobility improved. I was passionate enough about it to work harder than I needed to in order to accomplish my goals. The only excitement was when I hit a milestone—like the day I went to the TOSH swimming pool and walked in the water on my own, without any help, for the first time in two months—or when things went wrong.

One such "excitement" was the mysterious swelling of my knee. For some reason, my knee would balloon up with fluid and every three months I'd have to go into Dr. Trawick's office to have it taken care of. They'd stick a huge needle in my knee and suck all the fluid out and then pump my knee full of steroids. Gradually, over the course of a few months, the knee would swell back up. Dr. Trawick speculated that my body was not having it with the titanium screws and plates that were holding my knee and femur together. Some people can do fine with hardware in their body, and others can't tolerate it. It looked like I was in that second camp. My bones still needed time to heal, though, so Dr. Trawick didn't want to risk taking the hardware out before a year's time. So I had to power through the discomfort.

The swelling was made worse by working out, but I battled through it since I was so obsessed with my physical rehab. From the moment I got my walker, I pushed myself *hard*. Not only because I wanted to be able to walk normally again, but because the more I exercised, the sharper I was cognitively. That's true to this day. I'm particularly inspired by psychiatrist Dr. Norman Doidge, whose books (*The Brain That Changes Itself* and *The Brain's Way of Healing*) are filled with incredible stories of people, some of them brain-injured patients, overcoming their challenges with exercise. I was also inspired by Dr. Jill Bolte Taylor's book, *My Stroke of Insight*. Dr. Taylor describes in detail being conscious as she experiences a severe stroke that destroys portions of her left hemisphere. It helped me understand my own TBI and functioning despite major damage to the left side of my brain.

When I do go through a phase where my exercise lags, I don't feel as good about my emotional and mental well-being. When I'm exercising more, I feel sharper, and my memory, cognitive capacity, and self-esteem are better. Most everybody can understand the rush that comes from a good workout, but for brain injury survivors, it's even more crucial. Every brain injury survivor needs to find what works for them relative to their physical capacities.

Looking back, it's crazy how "normal" it seemed to have to go through a procedure of having a bunch of fluid sucked out of my knee and getting pumped up with a steroid. But there was just so much going on at the time, that seemed like an average day. The new norm was like nothing I'd ever have expected to go through. Fortunately, a year later, when Dr. Trawick performed the surgery to remove the titanium from my knee and femur, the procedure was a success. No more swelling.

While all this physical rehab was going on, I was also working with speech and occupational therapists. I remember telling Kim, my speech pathologist, in the early days that our work together was *the* most critical of all because it was going to help me function in life and get my job back. Relearning to speak, read, and write were my biggest obstacles in neuro rehab. I knew it and Kim knew it. Getting back to work was a huge incentive for me. She had me complete modules and specialized Internet speech therapy training that stretched my cognitive capacity.

In addition, three times a day, I would take a walk—first with my walker, then with a cane, and finally on my own steam—a block and a half down from our house to where the street dead-ended into a scenic overlook just above Salt Lake's Memory Grove Park. From that vantage, I could see out across the downtown area and the tower where the bank had its offices. I would stand there, looking out and wondering how my team was doing. I was desperate to get back, and I knew neuro rehab was the path.

Now, to give you a picture of just how tough this path was, it's important to remember that most TBI survivors don't *ever* make it back to a former high-level job, especially in cases as severe as mine. And I'm a three-time head case with nobody to blame but myself. The first time, back in my teens, when—thanks to a dare from one of my best friends—I skied a mogul run that was way above my skillset. I wrecked and (ironically) plowed into a "slow skiing" sign headfirst. I woke up in a toboggan, staring up at two ski patrolmen. The second head injury happened in Yorkshire, England, when I was in my early twenties and decided to have a go at racing bicycles down a hilly street. I missed a turn, clipped a guardrail, and smacked right into a cement lamppost. It's a miracle I wasn't killed. I woke up in a barracks-style hospital that looked like something out of World War Two, with a brain injury and broken bones all down the left side of my face. Helmets weren't yet in vogue. Sadly.

For most us survivors, if we do get a job, it's something that's low-stress or doesn't require specialized skills or knowledge. Or it's a volunteer gig or something we can do very part-time. In the years since my injury, I've met one person who went back to work as owner of a small business, but he was very upfront in saying that he'd handed off the day-to-day responsibilities to a trusted manager. I've also met a a few survivors who were very successful in IT coding and insurance sales who were able to capitalize on the functioning portions of their brains after they recovered. Given that my injury had knocked out some of the areas of my brain responsible for analytical thinking, nobody would have bet on me getting back to a full-time job as a senior management banker. Now, I didn't know any of this at the time. I had no idea that the odds were stacked so thoroughly against me. But, as my wife Laura says, "They don't know Greg."

Of course, in those early days of my recovery, work was out of the question. I wasn't even allowed to have my cell phone or look at my work email. Besides my iPad, which I used for brain games, I was full-on analog. My speech therapist set me up with a Franklin-style day planner like something straight out of the eighties. It was a black three-ring binder filled with pages for planning and journaling, and a calendar. I kept track of all of my appointments, goals, notes, accomplishments, and to-do lists. I wrote it all out by hand—and initially I had to use my left hand since my right hand was splinted. This day planner became an extension of me. I loved it. Laura told me later that I always had it with me. It was my safety net. If anyone asked me a question about my rehab that I couldn't answer, I could look it up. Or if I forgot a word when I had aphasia issues, I could look at my list of common words and verbs and pick a replacement.

Initially, each time I met with Kim, she tested me on my reading, speaking, and comprehension abilities, and I failed many of the tests. Later Kim reminded me they weren't "tests," just self-measurements so we could evaluate where I needed help and celebrate improvements. When I came into sessions, Kim would ask if I completed my homework from my last sessions, to which I always answered "yes." Then she asked if I remembered what we worked on from my last sessions, which I had difficulty with because my short-term memory sucked. I would BS my way through it, allowing neuroplasticity and brain remapping (which I didn't know anything about at the time) to give me clues as I remembered bits and pieces as I talked. The more I BS'd from small segments of my memory, the more the puzzle would start to crystalize, as neurons did their magic in my working brain cells. Living through this neuro-regenerative process is a real trip! I wasn't accustomed to failure, as I viewed it, so this motivated the hell out of me to keep working hard during and after each speech session.

Kim would have me build worksheets with common verbs and nouns to use in everyday speaking. I would say sentences using those words that would fit easily in my life. As I got better at it, I started to say banking terms. I know, go figure. Now I was being encouraged to use banking terms again when "loan presentation" used to be such a bad phrase for me. The biggest hurdle, was remembering the gist of those worksheets when I came back for my next session. Converting short to long-term memory is still one of my biggest weaknesses.

I drove myself to the limit almost every day. I got tired often and had to take hourly "brain breaks" to let my cranium rest. A brain break, I learned early on, was a quick five-minute rest that I tried to take once an hour. I would stop what I was doing, go to a quiet environment, take a quick nap, close my eyes, meditate, or sit in a state of mindfulness. This allows the brain to stop processing and just relax and breathe. In an intense situation, such as being at work or trying to learn something challenging, it's helpful to just walk away from it and let the brain and body relax. Doing this consistently, I could maintain energy longer and wasn't hit with fatigue as frequently or quickly as I would otherwise. If I didn't take brain breaks, I'd knock myself for a loop way early in the day. I could barely make it through the morning if I didn't take a few brain breaks. Fatigue was a daily event—it still is—and I could often be found catching an afternoon nap on the couch in the living room.

Since I still had to be monitored closely during this time, I would sometimes awake to find myself in the company of family members or the occasional friend who'd been recruited to watch over me. The unexpected benefit to this whole situation was that it brought me closer to my family. We had a lot of time to kill, and plenty of time to talk openly about anything. We have a "house rule" where, when we sit around the kitchen island, we can have candid conversation and "anything that's said on the island stays on the island." It's awesome. Plus, having family and friends take shifts with me allowed Laura to get in some sort of flow with life. She runs her own business, Hands On Promotions, selling customized promotional products, and she had to keep business afloat. At this point, she was much more attuned to the financial reality of our situation than I was.

My occupational therapist, Karen, helped me regain the skills to navigate daily life, but what I was most interested in was learning to drive again and getting my license back, and so I pestered Karen about this during most of my appointments that October. To me, the driver's license was a symbol of freedom and self-reliance. I felt like I was sixteen years old again. I studied hard at home for the written portion of the test, and I sat in my car in the garage and practiced moving my right foot back and forth between the gas and brake pedals and pressing hard on the brake. It was tough. This leg had just been shattered under a thousand pounds of Harley. It was now responsible for negotiating between the gas pedal and the stiff brake pedal on an older BMW. Physically, it was difficult to perform the actions that had been muscle memory for decades; you probably don't realize the complexity of motion and the nuances of movement that goes into what is likely an everyday action that you don't even have to think about.

My knee was raw, my skin was raw, and pressing on my big toe was raw. I had range of motion issues and tenderness all throughout. I didn't have full use of my big toe—the joint didn't bend all the way for a long time, probably for over a year. And I didn't have a toenail. It was gnarly. Dr. Bowen had stitched my big toenail onto my toe and it was later taken off by the team at IMC. It was a freakshow. I could see the scars on my toe from where the old toenail had been sewed on. It looked like Frankenstein's leg.

I pestered Karen for weeks to get ready for the test, which included an online written portion and a road test. You had to go through Karen to get to the test administrator, who was assigned specifically to the neuro rehab team at TOSH. What I didn't know at the time was that I was way ahead of schedule on this. But I wasn't just pestering—I also put in the work to regain the skills.

Braking was my biggest worry, since initially in my therapy sessions my foot shook when I lifted it. But it eventually became easier, and I was able to demonstrate to Karen, using a practice board with pedals on it that she kept in her office, that I could control the pedals and move back and forth easily enough. I drove with Laura in parking lots for a few weeks, and then it was time for my exam.

Emotionally, I'd just been in a full-on traumatic motorcycle accident. I'd seen the pictures from the scene of the accident and the hospital, and heard all the stories. I did have some fear about being on the road. It was something I used to do so easily, and now I had some nerves about it. All of that was cycling through my head as I was wondering if I could do it. But at the same time, I felt the freedom of driving as I practiced, just as I did when I was a teenager. I'd been cooped up in the hospital or on the couch for weeks. The thought of having a vehicle and being able to go where I wanted, when I wanted, gave me a sense of freedom and individualism and self-reliance. Independence was so close. Fingers crossed...

I took the road driving test at TOSH on November 15, three months after my Harley crash. My instructor sat next to me and Karen sat in back with one of her OT students from a local university. The car was full, but I wasn't nervous. I still had an inexplicable level of patience after waking up from the coma, which helped me stay calm in situations that would normally have made me anxious. The more I drove—very cautiously—during the road test—the more confident I became in my ability. I was hyper alert, always using my highest level of attention. When I would see a motorcyclist on the road, it would almost make me sick to my stomach, and so I had to manage those feelings while I was on the road with the instructor sitting next to me. I drove well through the suburbs of Murray and Sandy, and even on the freeway. I made it back to TOSH safely.

And... I passed! Whew! What an incredible relief.

Afterward, my instructor told me he fails many brain injury patients before they even leave the TOSH parking lot. I was glad he didn't tell me that *before* the exam. The road of rehab is long, but at least I'd made it back to the driver's seat.

73

17

One day that autumn, in the midst of all of this, Laura and I were out on our deck together, which is the happy place in our home. As you remember, when I was in the hospital, all I could think about was getting out and sitting on our terrace with a newspaper and cup of coffee.

The guy we bought our home from was a wood artisan and had access to unique pieces of wood from all over the world. A large company had ordered a load of gorgeous hardwood from the shop where Mark worked. But, the measurement was off by a fraction of an inch and it was returned. So, Mark purchased some of this hardwood and used it to construct what is probably the most intricately crafted home extension you could ever hope to host a barbecue on. Mark designed and handcrafted an inlaid box design for the floor, and guarded it with railings decorated with cutout designs that looked like a row of tulips. The deck has a second story, which partially serves as a roof to the lower terrace. The space has a hanging porch swing, strings of lights, and a speaker system.

This deck has always meant so much to me and Laura. It's a beautiful space for good times and free-flowing conversation with friends and family. It's a comforting space for us to have intimate, trust-building conversations with the beloved people in our life. Our safe place almost has a sacred quality to it, like it's infused with the spirit of our people. I associate it with good times.

That autumn day, Laura and I were relaxing on the deck, and from out of nowhere I started to feel intense remorse for the trauma we'd been through—for everything I'd put us through with the accident, when I should have known better than to ride when I was feeling sick. I felt like I'd done tremendous harm to Laura, our family, our friends, and myself. I felt guilt for the trauma Laura had experienced. I felt self-pity for all I'd lost and for all the rehab I was enduring. The reality of it all hit me. I began to sob uncontrollably. I was in anguish. It was as if I'd been protected from all of the negativity, inside of a bubble, and that bubble had abruptly popped.

When I shared this experience with Kim, my speech pathologist, she gave an incredible insight. Psychologically, the sadness meant my memory was starting to improve. Even though it felt awful, it was actually a good sign that my self-awareness was improving, which meant my brain was rebuilding itself. Experiencing the full range of human emotion was tangible evidence that rehab was working.

Still, it broke my heart to know Laura was hurting. She was suffering from post-traumatic stress, and it wasn't helping that I kept asking her to relive the trauma by asking her what had happened. She kept saying, "Greg, I've told you already. I've repeated myself many, many times. Our family has told you this many, many times." Laura was somber, grieving, and frustrated. And she felt guilty too, if you can believe it. She'd encouraged us to take the motorcycle trip, and felt partially at fault for my crash.

Despite my shaky memory, I remembered this moment well as one of my earliest memories from my time in room 1219. This pierced my awareness. Laura had saved me. She had been through hell to save me. I couldn't stand the idea that she could take any responsibility on herself. The biker's credo is that *if you get on a bike, that's on you.* Laura was already burdened enough as it was. Her mind was filled with graphic images during the same time I spent wrapped in a protected state of bliss, with no memory of the pain and horror. It wasn't fair. It was a dichotomy I couldn't reconcile—then or now. I knew I had to relieve Laura of the burden of being my memory-keeper. I had to do something.

* * *

Now, this chapter started out on the deck, but I want to take you inside and give you a tour of the house—I've got something I want you to see. The back deck on the first floor leads into the kitchen. To the left, you'll see my desk in the corner. To the right, you'll see the kitchen island where I ate my Frosted Flakes, and beyond that all of the appliances and counter space and whatnot. Through the kitchen is the living room and the stairs that lead up to our loft-style master bedroom and bathroom. The house at the time was filled with Stickley furniture—dark, heavy, expensive, masculine-looking stuff. Lots of leather and dark wood.

Mark had done extensive renovations. He'd taken a one-story bungalow, stripped out everything to the walls, and turned it into a two-story home in Frank Lloyd Wright's "arts and crafts" style, using all sorts of unique and rare pieces of wood all over the place—crown moldings, hardwood floors, wainscoting, trim around the windows.

Can you see it in your mind? Okay, now, go ahead and picture the place *covered* in hundreds of yellow sticky notes. Yes, sticky notes. Dotting all of the cupboards in the kitchen, the mirrors in the bathrooms, the walls, up the stairs, and next to my bed.

Written on those sticky notes were the details of my crash and recovery up to that point. Laura had gotten so tired of answering my questions over and over, she'd begun writing down the answers on sticky notes. That way, when I (inevitably) asked again about such-and-such event or person, she could say, "Check the bathroom mirror" or "Check the wall next to the couch." Or, I would see the notes when I woke up in the morning and made my way downstairs to get my cup of Joe, and I could revisit the story without even having to ask any questions. Done.

One by one, I took these sticky notes off the wall and transcribed them by hand into my black binder. I don't even remember doing this. But Laura says I'd copy each note and then crumple it up and throw it away, and that I was happy when I made progress. Every time I chucked a note, it was an achievement to celebrate. Little by little, I whittled away at the collection until the walls were clear. What's weird is that I don't remember a single sticky note. That's how bad my memory was back in the early days. But the sticky notes accelerated the process of relearning how to read and write.

The magical thing is, I didn't stop with sticky notes. Over time, I asked friends and family to recount their memories, and to send me copies of any emails, text messages, or social media posts they'd exchanged about the crash. Any pictures they'd taken or collected during that time.

A couple months after that, I got it in my head that I wanted to know what the doctors and other medical staff had said. I collected every bit of information I could find: medical charts, x-rays, scans, and rehabilitation notes from Life Flight, Kootenai Health, and Intermountain Medical Center. I tracked down the police report and news stories. Jimmy says I was like an archaeologist, digging through the past and trying to piece it all together. He says I seemed to feel relief when I was able to regurgitate this thing on paper. I imagine I did.

I don't recall having any sort of clear intention at the time except for that I had a strong desire to reconstruct the story of a "lost" month of my life and to capture the memories so I'd never forget. I didn't realize it would someday morph into this very book you're reading right now.

Owning my story made me feel more in control of it. At that time in my life, I had control of almost *nothing*. I felt lost. I didn't have purpose. I didn't have many friends around; I couldn't really be a dad or a husband at that time; nobody was relying on me. Instead, I was relying on everybody else, especially in those first few months. My sense of self was obliterated, and I wasn't in control of my destiny. This was extremely out of the ordinary for me; I started working at the bank during my senior year in high school and left home for college after I graduated. I wasn't used to depending on others. I'd always been the go-to, take-charge guy. Now I was ... what? I didn't know.

But I had a few things to call my own: I had my comfy leather couch in the living room, I had my iPad for Brain Games and my black binder. Eventually I hit the big time and got to have a cordless phone next to me on the coffee table—though at first it didn't occur to me to pick it up and call anyone. Just knowing I had a landline gave me some sense of independence. As inconsequential as it seems, that black binder was mine, and it felt great to have ownership of something. Writing down my experience in my binder allowed me to quit relying on others when I couldn't access my memory.

Time and again I'd cycle through a pattern: I would ask Laura (or whomever) a question. They would answer the question and tell me that I'd already asked it many times before. I would experience the very jarring and disturbing sensation of realizing that I was missing memories of my own life. And then I'd forget, and the whole cycle would begin again.

Eventually, as my short-term memory improved, I had my wits about me enough to realize that, if I didn't write down what someone said—like, *right this instant*—I'd lose it. Especially with Laura, after I'd grasped how incredibly painful it was for her to keep reliving the horror, I knew what was being said to me was precious.

My earliest memory of writing is rushing to write down something that she'd said. I remember grabbing my black binder and having tears in my eyes, trying to figure out how to write such-and-such word or put a few words together. It was agony, trying to get it onto paper before it evaporated from my short-term memory. It was painfully frustrating when I couldn't figure it out, but I couldn't give up. I was driven by an absolute *need*. I didn't want to have to ask anybody ever again. That became an obsession to me: to never forget. Writing it down, it became crystalized and tangible.

Common wisdom in the medical community is that, when it comes to relearning skills after TBI, time is of the essence. Medical personnel frequently tell survivors and caregivers that the bulk of recovery is gained within the first six to twelve months—and then it plateaus.

All my life I've been given goals from people at higher levels than me, whether in school or in my career. I see those as targets delivered "top down" to me. Well, okay. I see those as expectations from an exterior source. I take them for what they're worth, but they've always been secondary to my own expectations for myself, and my own goals that I set internally. And the goals I set for myself have always been so much higher than those set by other people. So, even though I didn't have my wits about me and didn't totally understand it—I was in a blissful state, filled with love, happiness, and care, and surrounded by euphoria. Somebody expressed some arbitrary limitations for me and I just set it aside and didn't let it faze me. I just kept working as hard as I could. Their timeframes or boundaries didn't drive me. They were meaningless. A non-issue. Other people's expectations were nothing but noise.

I felt an ungodly pressure to remap my brain and recover, and I was starting from scratch. Case in point: as you recall, when Laura handed me the newspaper during my half-day pass to read on our deck, I found myself looking at a garbled mess of letters and realized my ability to read was lost. I knew I had a long way to go, but I was still experiencing my blissful state of calm, so I wasn't bugging out—it was just surreal. Fortunately, my obsession was a major accelerant. Eventually the writing process would prove to be a major recovery tool. Wow, it strapped rocket boosters to my cognitive abilities. Things started to come back to me as I wrote, and the more I did it, the faster and faster I progressed in reading, writing, and speaking.

Eventually, I got my electronics back and began typing up some of my handwritten notes. At first, it was just a timeline of facts, but then my family reminded me of funny or heartening anecdotes from that time, and I even saw some warm human touches in the medical notes.

And so, what began as a chronology of events became something more and evolved naturally. Then I put a title on it. I called it "Warmth and a Bad Fish." And with that, it became something I wanted to share.

I felt burdened by a huge debt. I'd been given so many gifts as a result of my accident and had received so much love and support and kindness from everyone around me. I wanted to do something to give back, and I thought sharing my story could help other survivors and caregivers. I wasn't really thinking of it as a proper "memoir" at that time. I was a banker, not an author. It was just my story and my timeline, and I wanted to share it and help other survivors overcome the same obstacles I dealt with.

I was a bit naïve and still wore my rose-colored glasses, but I thought people would like to read it. And frankly, it was the only thing I had to give. All told, it took about a year to get it together. I added some pictures, printed out copies, handwrote a personal note on the front of each copy, signed it, and put it in a binder. I gave copies to friends, family, and some of the medical professionals who'd helped me. Looking back, it seems like a pretty lame way of saying "thank you," but it's all I had.

18

O ne of the many things I obsessed about after my accident was getting back to work. I constantly wondered what my team was up to, and urgently wanted to get my life back on track. Early in my recovery, I received a check from MetLife for long-term disability. The amount was about forty or fifty percent of my salary. It shook me to receive that check. I didn't consider myself disabled even though I had significant issues, and it never occurred to me that I wouldn't return to work. I asked Laura to drive me to the MetLife office in Murray, and I went in and asked to speak with their director.

When he came to the waiting area, I handed him the check I'd received. I told him I wasn't disabled, and I asked him to take me off the long-term disability list. I gave up my safety net. Looking back, I'll bet he was thinking, "Sure I'll take your check back. Are you serious? What an idiot!" My pride and ego were showing that day.

It didn't occur to me that I might not get back to work as a senior vice president, or, if I did, that I might not perform well in my job. It was only years later that I found out that my physicians and therapists in neuro rehab never expected me to return to my senior management position at the bank.

After seeing the reduced income that I would have gotten on long-term disability, I thought I needed to return to my job in order for us to keep our house and lifestyle. And I needed to get back fast.

Now, Laura and I were in a luckier position than many people who find their lives suddenly and completely upended by TBI. Just before the accident, we'd sold our boat that we kept at Lake Powell—and the check cleared while I was in a coma. My Harley was totaled in the accident and our insurance reimbursed us for the full cost plus the cost of all the Harley gear I was wearing when I crashed. Laura sold her Low Rider after I was flown back to Salt Lake. We were out of debt except for the mortgage on the house. And while I realize I was extremely lucky to even have access to long-term disability benefits, I didn't want to take them. It was hard on my pride—and on my sense of identity. I wanted to get back to work. I was a banker, dammit!

My getting back to work was important to Laura too, and so from the moment it became clear in Idaho that I'd survive the crash, she helped grease the skids for my professional return. Of course, at that time, we had no idea where I'd land in terms of my cognitive recovery, so Laura played it safe. She basically put things on lockdown. Anybody who wanted to see me had to go through Laura. She put a sign on the door of my room at IMC saying that anyone who wanted to visit me should check with Laura first for access. She blocked everyone. She didn't want to let people know I was experiencing extreme aphasia and my memory was shot to hell. She kept her cards close to her vest. All she would say was, "You can't see Greg. This isn't a good time."

After I'd returned home and had rehabbed to a point where I could maintain a minimum of lucid conversation, Laura hosted a lunch at our house for my team from the bank. She wanted them to see that I was on the road to recovery. She also wanted to do something that would make me feel good, since I'd been pestering the crap out of her to check up on my group and see how they were doing.

The luncheon went supremely well, and Laura was convinced that my cognitive function reached an acceptable level. She took an unbelievably bold move and hosted a lunch for the bank's executives, including my boss. I vaguely remember feeling pumped for these lunches, since it felt great to be with my work friends, and also a bit anxious about my ability to remember names and to talk okay. The lunches were awkward and stressful and great all at the same time. I could rally and bring my A-game for a short time, and Laura used her social skills as a flaming extrovert to keep things flowing. But being with my colleagues was one thing and being with the bosses was another. It took every ounce of my cognitive ability to gather my executive functioning and demonstrate that I could communicate as a senior management banker. Mentally and physical, I paid the price. Fatigue blasted me like Thor's hammer. But being back with my colleagues was worth it.

Getting me back to work was a big goal for the both of us, though we each had our own motivations. For Laura, financial security was and is a big deal. Her dad, when he was alive, was unbelievably successful in commercial real estate, but he had bipolar disorder. He'd make a bunch of money and then spend it all, and he ended up dying early with nothing. She'd also supported herself and three kids for years as a single mother. So, Laura had seen financial insecurity up close and wanted to get back to a stable place as soon as possible.

My personal motivations were different from Laura's—and "new" Greg had a *way* different attitude than old Greg. Old Greg was all about climbing the career ladder. He was materialistic, and loved buying expensive toys for himself and the family. For the new me, getting back to work was about the money, for sure—especially as I began to grasp the financial realities of our situation—but it was more so about identity and connection. I missed my people and I missed my role as "Banker Bob." I grew up at the bank. I'd met some of my best friends there, including Laura. It was my second home, and I couldn't wait to get back. I was lucky and grateful that I had a job waiting for me. Harris, the Bancorporation's CEO, called Laura shortly after the accident and assured her my job would be waiting for me when I got back. He said, "Laura, the last thing I want you to worry about right now is Greg's job."

On November 16th, the day after I passed my driving test, I attended the lunch portion of my region meeting at the bank's training center. This was a monthly meeting of the three hundred members of our region, and I used to conduct it with my colleague Brad. Brad was my counterpart at the bank—he managed the retail side of our region while I directed the commercial function.

Brad was awesome. He was the most supportive partner you could ever hope for. I knew if I needed him, I could call and he'd be there at a moment's notice—and I would do the same for him. We managed the region together and were tied at the hip, so to speak. We were partners, but more importantly, our bond was tight. We gave each other crap, which made working together fun. And we'd both been in each other's shoes in our banking careers. I grew up in retail and Brad spent time as a successful commercial lender and manager. We would jump into each other's roles when needed and it was a riot showing our region members I could do his job and vice versa. It was natural for Brad to jump in and manage my team after my crash.

I arrived at our region management meeting with Lori, a friend and fellow executive at the bank. She graciously picked me up from home to give me the VIP transport service. Her presence was calming and helped me feel more confident returning to a work setting. She helped me get my head right as we drove. She said, "Greg, you've presented to your region team hundreds of times. This is nothing to you. Remember, you're the comic relief guy. Just say a few words about being grateful to be back and I'll get you out of there."

I walked into the large conference room with a cane. Weird. It was surreal being back in this familiar environment but being so changed. They let me speak for a few minutes just after the lunch break. I told them about my coma-awakening "WTF" moment. That got a laugh.

When I was in the hospital in a coma, Brad had held a moment of silence at our region meeting. I later heard about all the team members who sent cards and said they were praying for me. Tears flowed as I told them how grateful I was and what a gift and honor it was to be able to stand and speak to them—especially since I had just relearned how to talk again. Many members of our region lined up to hug me and say they were extremely grateful I survived and was recovering well. Even the most introverted of our region team hugged me. The ones you couldn't get "word one" out of. How did that happen in a banking environment? It felt like such an incredible gift to receive so much warmth from my work colleagues.

My occupational and speech therapies were crucial to my getting back to work, and it was up to my speech pathologist (Kim), occupational therapist (Karen), and my neuro rehabilitation specialist (Dr. Dodds) to give me the official okay to return to my job. As part of my occupational therapy, Karen had me bring my HP 12-C finance calculator to one of my sessions. Laura picked it up from my office and I practiced with my son Josh for a few days at home. I was able to show Karen I could calculate mortgage payments and amortization schedules. I also asked Brenda, my assistant at the bank, to make copies of loan presentations I'd approved over the past year so I could start getting familiar with the work I used to do.

Kim was responsible for managing my cognitive rehab and fatigue, which she reported directly to Dr. Dodds. Between the two of them, they would decide if or when I had the capacity to handle complex work flow, speech, and writing, and how much impact it would have on my energy levels and memory. In other words, how much work could I handle without damaging myself or hindering the improvements I was making. They knew if I worked too hard, too fast, I could spiral and go backward in a hurry. Toward the end of November, she and Dr. Dodds gave me the go-ahead. I was to start at just two hours a week and scale up over the course of a few months, increasing an hour or two a week, with Dr. Dodds' approval, with the intention of returning to full-time eventually if I could handle it. I found out years later that Kim and Dr. Dodds were very concerned and doubtful that I could handle my fulltime senior management position. The bank's HR team and my boss signed off on my planned schedule.

I started back to work on Monday, November 28th. I was beyond grateful to be back after only three and a half months, which was way ahead of any expectations. A funny thing I didn't learn until later was that my boss, John, had managed to get past Laura's velvet rope at IMC and visit me in my room, but—thank god—I apparently managed to hold myself together enough to *not* blow my chances of getting back to work. I don't remember his visit, much less what I may have said during our conversation, but much later, I asked him why he'd allowed me to rejoin the team. He told me that he knew I wouldn't allow myself to come back to work unless I was ready. It warms me to know I'd built a strong foundation of trust with Harris and John and the other executives at the bank but looking back I know I wasn't in a particularly sound place to be judging my own abilities. I barely had my wits about me, but I thought I was a rock star. I was confident I could relearn my banking skills just like I had relearned to speak, read, and write.

My first day back, I walked into my office and saw that Brad had a new nameplate made for me. "Beuford Nordfelt." And as if that weren't enough, they bought a colorful purple fish and had it in a new hourglass type fish bowl. They named it—you guessed it—Beuford. I couldn't stop laughing that morning. I asked them to take a picture of me with my new nameplate and fish. My team laughed too and it broke the ice of me being back in my management role with a new identity and fresh fish.

What I hadn't fully realized at the time was that getting back to work was one thing, but actually *doing* the work was a whole different matter. I was in way over my head from an analytical perspective. I could present myself in a way that made it appear that I was good to go because of my accelerated rehab. People thought I was more functional, from an executive perspective, than I really was. My analytical abilities had not yet been rehabilitated.

In my role as director of commercial lending for my region at the bank, I made lending decisions for companies generating multimillion dollars in revenue. What came across my desk were loan presentations that had pages upon pages of analysis and recommendations, and it was my job to sift through all this detailed information and determine whether the loan could be approved or not.

I had my own personal lending limit. If it was above mine, I could combine with another credit officer or submit to the senior loan committee. I had to find any holes, and any missing or incorrect information. We had a method for calculating a business's risk of failing from a financial standpoint, and the method combined three or four different elements of risk into a spreadsheet. These spreadsheets were incredibly complicated and used formulas to talk to each other; the formulas traveled from one spreadsheet to the other to the other to the other. And then they built reports from these multiple, complex spreadsheets. Lots of number data went into them—financial statements, tax returns, forecasts, etc. We used this data to create risk grades based on federal regulation, which were used to determine how risky it would be to make multimillion-dollar loans. The complexity of this number crunching and risk analysis process was at the highest level of what commercial bankers use. Long story short, this was left-brain heaven.

When I was at my peak, I could take a brief look at some financials and forecasts, have a discussion with the company's CEO or CFO, and have a pretty good idea before lunch was over whether we'd be able to chase a deal for a few million dollars. I could attend a hundred-million-dollar bank group syndication meeting in New York and know whether to pursue a participation in the project after leaving the conference, before I got to the elevator.

After the TBI, I would look at these same types of complex data and stare in a state of confusion, shock, and trepidation—it was an awakening to see how hard it would be to relearn everything. I knew that I could do it, that I'd done it—and done it well—in the past, but I didn't know how I was going to relearn it. Initially, "overwhelming" doesn't even come close to describing my situation. It would have been horrific if my rose-colored glasses weren't smoothing my perception of the enormity of my "up shit creek without a paddle" predicament. I don't think that I could have handled the emotional and psychological panic of this situation today—in fact, I know I couldn't. But at the time, I handled the turmoil with unbelievable calm.

I felt blissful, loving, kind, and happy. So, I had to have been spending time in my "safe place" in order to make it through this.

Fortunately, neuroplasticity was doing its remapping without me realizing it or forcing it to happen. I had to come up with my own creative, right-brain system to deal with the loss of my analytical left brain. As I continued to work through Excel and our systems day after day, images began to materialize as I maneuvered between one sheet to the next. Without knowing it, my creative self was assigning a little animal or symbol to differentiate each worksheet. Numbers were getting colors and I was teaching myself how to navigate the complexities of what was once so natural to me. My right hemisphere and neuroplasticity was kicking ass and taking names, helping me relearn my senior management job. Describing this with the English language does not do it justice. It was on the verge of magical. Without it, I wouldn't have been able to understand numbers or keep track of where I was within the complexities of our loan presentation risk-analysis system. Of course, I kept this to myself. It was a secret system. The thought of discussing it with anyone never came to me. It was a nonissue. It was the new me.

At first, when I was doing the two-hour stints, I was still experiencing my state of bliss and had no idea what I was up against. I was in my happy place and glad to be amongst friends and to have made it back to work. But weeks down the road, when I had to start actually doing the work and when I was in meetings with our chief credit officer, it dawned on me. Brad attended those meetings with me and helped me pick up the slack. In general, he and our assistant, Brenda, carried me through. I was smart enough to have our chief lending officer make big lending decisions for me. They all protected me through the initial stages.

The way the office was laid out, Brad's office and Brenda's cubicle flanked either side of a hallway that led to my office. If someone turned left in front of Brad's office, they had to walk past Brenda and down about ten feet to get to my office. I was in a secluded spot, all by myself at the end of the hallway. It was actually a bit of a lonely place, but it was the perfect setting for someone recovering from a TBI. Brenda served as a literal gatekeeper. She stopped anyone from going down the hallway and would ask, "Do you have an appointment?"

I didn't realize it at the time, but Brad had assigned her to not let anybody into my office unless they were family or someone he trusted. I suspect he was worried that anybody who interacted with me would have a different opinion of me than they'd had before. They'd be comparing new Greg with old Greg. So, I was sitting back in there, in seclusion, working my butt off to relearn everything that Banker Bob used to do—all the stuff that Dr. Dodds later told me no one expected me to be able to do. Brad and Brenda played a major part in protecting me—not to mention doing the work themselves that I wasn't yet capable of doing—so I could take the time to relearn my job from my right-brain perspective now that my left brain was offline. The first month was a bit fuzzy. I don't remember much of what I accomplished, but I was driven to figure a way around my deficits.

In January 2012, I got a dose of reality that really kicked my motivation into high gear: our human resources representative explained that my leave benefits—sick days, vacation, FMLA (Family Medical Leave Act) days—would run out toward the end of February 2012. My partner in HR was awesome—she helped me calculate that leave down to the day, and always kept in good contact with me to make sure I was up-to-date on my status and understood what my options were. I had to get back to full-time hours by February 22nd or else I'd be downgraded to a part-time employee. This would have negative ramifications on compensation and benefits, including my health insurance, which I absolutely couldn't allow to happen, especially since I returned my long-term disability check to MetLife (in hindsight, a pretty stupid move, but I've always been drawn to high-pressure situations). The heat was on.

As far as getting the go-ahead to return to work full-time, there were a lot of hands in the proverbial pot. It wasn't just a matter of me be willing to do it—because, believe me, I was willing. The bank had to be sure I was competent to perform the work. Kim and Dr. Dodds, on the other hand, needed to be sure that going back to full-time status wouldn't compromise my recovery. They were assessing not only my competency but my well-being. They needed to be sure that the stress wouldn't send my rehabilitation into a tailspin.

If survivors push themselves too hard, we can blow up our recovery. We can experience sensory overload, depression, and eventually burnout—which is a sure path to giving up completely. For months, I walked a tightrope between maintaining my well-being and pushing myself enough to get fully back to work.

Even though people thought I was fully "back" within a few months, the truth of the matter is that it took almost a year of intense work to relearn all of the aspects of the analytical side of my banking job. However, despite my awakening and initial sense of shock at what I couldn't do, I don't ever remember thinking that I couldn't relearn it. I knew that I used to know this stuff like the back of my hand, and I was confident that I could get to a certain level of analytical skill, but I knew I'd never fully regain the peak capacity all of it.

The reality is, there are certain aspects of my brain that are offline. And because I knew the reality and accepted it, I wasn't afraid of it. So when the day came that I realized I'd reached a place that was as good as it was going to get, I was okay with that. Part of what kept me so sanguine about my limitations in the analytical area is that I was rocking it in terms of my people skills. I'd come out of the crash and the coma with a huge gift for connecting with people and empathizing with their emotions. The right and left sides, the orientation toward people and analysis, they were in complement. I had clarity in understanding that what my mind had rebuilt itself to be was in itself beauty. It was all good.

I eventually got to a place in my job where I was doing things better than ever. I was working from a place that I didn't have access to before. I was actually having successes *because* of the brain injury. I taught myself to use my right brain to do most of the analytical stuff that my left brain used to do, but I also had a new level of access to a creative and personal side. I could connect with people like never before. I understood my team's personal needs and motivations, and used that new understanding to support them in crushing their goals. I even helped a couple people move to positions in the company that they were better suited for. I couldn't believe what I was doing. I would never have known how much my interpersonal skills influenced how we worked together and how we handled customers and assessed risk.

My team was firing on all cylinders. Between Brad and I, we had the largest, highest-performing region in all of Utah and Idaho. We weren't just hitting our goals—we were blowing them away. I was used to exceeding goals, but people couldn't believe I'd just gotten out of a coma and there I was, back and producing at an extremely high level.

Today, looking back, the "new Greg" knows that "2011 Greg" was screwed—if you don't mind me putting it bluntly. For the first couple of years, my rose-colored glasses prevented me from seeing there was any problem with how I was operating. I was happy. Happy to be back at work. Happy to be relearning. Feeling love and warmth and connection with everyone in my world. I really understood what incredible gifts and tools I'd been given thanks to my TBI. My immense gratitude overshadowed any of the overwhelm I may have felt about any obstacles I had to overcome.

If I felt any sadness during that time period, it wasn't for myself; it was for Laura. I kept asking myself, "How am I going to help Laura? How am I going to keep our marriage together?"

19

While I was doing my thing with rehab and writing my book and starting back to work, Laura finally had a minute to breathe. She was working hard to find her own semblance of normalcy. In addition to the challenge of having her entire life upended, Laura was experiencing severe post-traumatic stress.

At first, Laura's post-traumatic stress expressed itself in shock, horror, and disbelief. She was trying to get a grip on what she'd just seen. When that initial phase passed, it morphed into extreme sadness and mourning—including mourning for the loss of my former self and our former relationship. She was unable to accept the new reality. There were a lot of tears. The post-traumatic stress was exacerbated by having to answer my constant questions. She was demanded to repeat the story, while at the same time never wanting to talk about it again. She was also fielding questions from family, friends, work colleagues, insurance companies, doctors, and the Harley Davidson dealership. From everyone. It just seemed endless, like she couldn't get away from it.

She was sick of discussing the accident—with me or anybody else—and got really tired of people asking how I was. People always asked, "How's Greg doing?" and nobody ever asked "How are *you* doing, Laura?" Caregivers are forgotten. This happened to Laura, and it happens to others, starting right in the hospital emergency room. Medical professionals rush in for the survivor, all the focus is on the survivor, and caregivers are left feeling like a piece of furniture. Only if there's a death is the caregiver surrounded by therapists.

Laura rarely voiced her frustrations, but they expressed themselves. She could have a short temper and was just generally mad at the world. In the middle of a conversation, she would reach a breaking point. "I can't talk about this anymore," she'd say abruptly during one of my rounds of questioning. But I'd forget we'd had the conversation and I'd come back and ask it again. So, early on, Laura was trying to back away from a situation that she couldn't back away from, because myself and others were forcing her to relive it. Post-traumatic stress is generally thought to need an outlet, but this may have been too much of a good thing.

In the early aftermath of my accident, Laura's attention was focused on me and my very acute needs. But finally, when the dust settled and her post-traumatic stress symptoms persisted, she sought therapy. It didn't go well. The first therapist wanted Laura to relive her childhood, which was awful. After her mother divorced Laura's father, she moved Laura and her siblings from Utah to Chicago to live with her new husband's five boys. Laura was a lost soul in a huge family. And her stepfather proved himself to be abusive, verbally and physically. Laura had no interest in dredging up the past in therapy when she was there to get over her post-traumatic stress. She says, "It was like throwing gas on a fire in an attempt to put the fire out." The second therapist had a mindfulness-based approach that was heavy on the meditation. Laura didn't find herself connecting with that. Two attempts were enough, and it put her off the whole thing. When Laura doesn't want to face something, she buries it. Her upbringing, her first marriage, this accident. She just wanted it to go away. She wanted to put it behind her and move forward.

Laura's difficulties were heightened by a sense of aloneness. Months into this ordeal, she was wondering "Where *is* everybody?" Before the accident, we had tons of friends, been involved in all sorts of activities and communities–especially Laura, the flaming extrovert—and now it was eerily quiet. Three or four months after the accident, a friend of ours named Heidi asked if she could drop something off at our house and Laura said, "Of course! We haven't seen you guys. Where are you?" and Heidi said, "You sent out a message on Facebook saying 'Please give us time to heal.' We took that seriously—we didn't want to bother you." Laura said, "Heidi! We didn't mean *you*." But Heidi said, "We, all of your friends, took it to heart as applying to all of us."

This was an awakening moment for Laura. With her instinct to circle the wagons and protect us from intruders, she had unwittingly turned away folks whose support and friendship we really needed. No wonder things had gone so quiet. In general, both Laura and I are inclined to put off help. For the most part, the friends and family who helped us did so by pushing their way in. If someone asked if they could help, she'd say no. She kept saying "I'm good" when she was in fact not good at all. "I was in terrible shape," she later admitted. "I was in a cocoon of my own, just like Greg was in his coma. Greg was not really 'here' for a long time, and I was in a really bad place but didn't want to admit that to anybody. I had too much pride. I just kept saying, 'No, I'm fine.' But I was in a state of overwhelm. Life kept going on, things kept waiting for me—the yard, the cooking—and I didn't get that it was okay to ask for help." Of course, to the people close to us, Laura's condition was apparent.

When she resisted their help, they "got around" her by just doing, working off the principle of "It's better to ask forgiveness than permission." Our next-door neighbors at the time, Aaron and Kim, mowed our lawn and brought in our garbage cans. Aaron didn't ask "Do you need it?" He's a fellow adrenaline junkie who knows what it's like to bust up his body, and so when he heard about what I'd gone through, he just took it upon himself to help.

Once, though it was very out of character for her, Laura confided in one of her old friends, someone she'd known since high school, and admitted that she was struggling—which is putting it lightly—with the caregiver role. Struggling with my new personality, struggling with all of the responsibility.

Laura's friend's husband had also suffered a TBI in a motorcycle crash, so Laura thought she was in a safe place confiding with her. Her friend responded with these words: "Suck it up." It took Laura aback and hurt her deeply, but she didn't know how to handle it. This woman was and still is a close friend, and Laura was reluctant to lose or damage the friendship, so she just let the whole incident pass. But this callous sentiment, expressed so casually, scarred Laura. She'd already been having a difficult time confiding in others about the struggle she was experiencing, and this incident put a nail in the coffin *for years*. Literally, years. But, while it may seem inconceivable that someone would tell Laura to "suck it up," in all fairness, Laura hadn't told anybody how severe my injuries were. Relatively few people knew. Laura underrepresented the extent of my injuries in a big, big way. For years.

It didn't come out until we started publicly speaking about how to nurture relationships after brain injuries and admitted all the mistakes we made. As we were more open and honest with others, word started to get out about how serious my accident was and the impact it had on Laura. People started asking "Why didn't you tell us?" "Why didn't you ask for help?" Nobody knew how bad it really was, including members of our family.

About that same time, Netflix released a critically acclaimed documentary called *My Beautiful Broken Brain*. A British documentary producer, Lotje Sodderland, filmed the movie primarily with her iPhone after waking up from her serious brain bleed that almost killed her. The documentary shows the aftermath of surviving a brain injury and what it's like to recover and go through the neuro rehabilitation process. As a documentary producer, it came naturally to Lotje to pick up the iPhone and start taking video. Since the story is filmed by a survivor, from her own perspective, it was invaluable to me. There's not a lot of media out there created by survivors, and so this movie was precious to me. I became obsessed with watching it over and over. The movie changed my realization of my own recovery.

When Laura watched the film, her perspective changed dramatically. She said, "Honey, after five years, I finally understand how you feel when the family comes over and it's loud and confusing with all the grandkids." She realized I was struggling more than she thought and knew why. Laura and our kids didn't know the extent of what I was handling, and how that affected my ability to relate with them in the ways we normally did—which was as a big group. We liked seeing all six kids and our sixteen (and counting) grandkids together under one roof. Whenever we had gatherings, it was natural that we'd want to get everyone together. The problem is, big families make a lot of noise. Our home is relatively small—smaller than the suburban home we raised the family in. And with hardwood floors, and the fact that there are only a few doors, except on the bathrooms, noise travels. It's okay in the summertime because the kids can play outdoors, but when the weather is bad and we host our entire family, things get overwhelming *fast*.

We encouraged our kids to watch *My Beautiful Broken Brain* so they could see what living with a TBI is like for me. I don't want my family to think I don't love being around them, and this movie gave them some insight into how and why I have to modify my interaction to allow for the challenges I face. The movie gave us a way to communicate about my sensitivities to noise, activity, crowds, fatigue and bright lights. I try my best to power through uncomfortable situations, but we have to work around the TBI as a family. For example, we have dinners together, and if we're at one of our kids' houses, I'll sometimes take a second car in case I have to leave early. Or, the grandkids will be asked to quiet down or to play in the basement or outside.

It has an impact on everybody, and I'm sure there are times when people are frustrated or disappointed. Despite the downer of my getting easily overwhelmed and tired, I love our children and grandkids, and I try to find ways to show my love despite the fact that I can't handle the noise and confusion as well as I used to. In the early days of my recovery, holding our newborn grandbabies was a healing experience. I'd sit in a chair with an infant snuggled on my chest, both of us snoozing. Now, I especially value the moments when I can break away from the crowd and connect one-on-one with our family members. That lets us find a bit of intimacy and really get to know each other better. I shine in one-on-one conversations, and those internal connections are more readily available to me. It's up to me to make that happen, independent of the bustling setting.

Whether it's with one of our kids, one of their spouses, or one of our grandkids, it feels incredibly fulfilling to me. It's one of the ways I've come to terms with what I can't do and focus instead on what I can do.

20

As you can imagine, everything that was going on put a strain on my relationship with Laura. This scared me. In one of my early therapy sessions, I was told that around seventy-five percent of marriages end in divorce when a spouse experiences a TBI. And I sure as hell didn't want to be part of that statistic.

Laura is everything to me. My marriage and keeping my family together immediately became my first priority, but I only had so much attention to go around.

My second priority was rehab and relearning the basics of speaking, reading, and writing, and walking again. I was obsessed with it—I had to be in order to get my job back and some sense of identity. Then, when I was back at work, the bank was getting the best of me. I spent every ounce of energy focusing on showing my best self to the outside world. Everything else was collateral damage. When I got home at night from work, I would absolutely crash. Just pass out on my rehab couch. I'd marshaled all of my resources to get through the workday and had nothing left. Laura was understandably upset and resentful that she was getting the scraps. Once, after an exhausting day at work, she said to me: "The bank is getting the best part of you." It was yet another moment of awareness and awakening for me.

And it wasn't just that I was strapped for mental and physical resources. Our relationship was also strained by the fact that, after the accident, I was guided by a new set of motivations and desires.

Before the accident, my life was motivated by two questions: *What can I buy? And what can I jump off of?* Laura and I worked our asses off as hard as we could so that we could play as hard as we could. We both had an insatiable thirst for travel and outdoor adventure—motorcycling, boating, scuba diving, skiing, sports—and we worked hard in order to be able to afford it for ourselves and our family. Our shared love of adventure was one of the bonds that made our marriage and family thrive.

Now, I'm not like that anymore. I don't feel a drive for adventure as much as I feel a drive for heartfelt experiences, whether at home or traveling. Plus, I was already pushing my luck having survived three TBIs. My neurologists told me I shouldn't have survived my third traumatic brain injury, and I definitely wouldn't survive a fourth. Continuing the adrenaline-junkie lifestyle would kill me. They knew it, and in my heart, I knew it too. My risk-taking days were over. For Laura and I, this meant that some of our shared activities were off the table now, which sucked in the worst way. Egging each other on was a big part of our dynamic. How would we replace it? Laura was already grieving the loss. So was I.

Plus, my personality had undergone some substantial changes after the brain injury. One of my best friends, David, who I met when we started working together at the bank in the late eighties, has been with me through thick and thin on both sides of the motorcycle accident. David is like my brother, we're that close. He knows me better than just about anybody. And so when I asked him to describe the changes he'd seen in me, he didn't mince words. He said I used to be a loud, aggressive, "kick ass and take names" kind of guy who wasn't afraid to get a little bit nasty when I needed to be. Luckily for me, David was willing to tolerate my obnoxious traits because we had such a heartfelt connection and for the most part, I was a stand-up guy and he trusted me. Now, he says, the "alpha dog" side of me has diminished and the softer side has become more pronounced.

Whereas before I'd been a totally left-brained, analytical-thinking Banker Bob, now I'm right-brained. Even now, years later, I'm still maturing into my new identity as a right-brainer. I have access to more of that hemisphere than I ever did before, and it's changed the way I operate. It used to be that, when faced with a decision, it was analysis first, feelings second. Now, it's the opposite. I'm also more creative now. When we first moved into our home, Laura gave me a couple walls to call my own in our basement, and I put up some certificates and sports memorabilia and called it good. After the crash, I was cutting out pages from the Pottery Barn catalog and putting them on Laura's desk as a subtle hint for home-decorating ideas. It wasn't uncommon for her to ask, "Greg, who are you and what the hell have you done with my husband?"

There's a lot of beauty and enlightenment to be experienced through the right brain, but it wasn't the brain orientation I was raised with and trained to handle, starting with my parents and teachers in early childhood, on up through everything I'd learned and faced over the course of my forty-nine years. All of a sudden, I found myself with unfettered, untrained access to my right brain, and it was like unleashing the Kraken. I hadn't been taught the rules and boundaries of how to operate maturely from a dominant right brain. It was like I'd been trained to use a calculator, and all the sudden someone took away the calculator and replaced it with a paint set. Now I've got a paint set as my primary tool, and I wasn't trained to paint. So, in some ways I've made quite a mess.

One of the most surprising and incredible side effects of the near-death experience was that it healed an intense anger and hatred I'd held in my heart. Before the accident and the coma, I'd lost both parents, my sister, and my brother— all within a four-year period. It damaged me. I was profoundly hurting. I hated God and the universe for taking my loved ones away from me.

Losing my parents had thrown me for a loop. In part it was because I'd never really acknowledged that their death was an event that was going to take place, even as they were telling me and my siblings to take sticky notes and put our names on their belongings around their house. I couldn't participate. It frustrated me that we were even talking about their death, even though my parents—who were always big plan-makers—had the arrangements all in writing. None of it should have come as a surprise to me, but I refused to acknowledge it. So, when it happened, it crushed me.

For a while, it was my dad who was barely hanging on. He had serious medical issues and was in and out of the hospital. But it was actually my mom who went first. She was eighty-two and had some medical issues, but nothing that seemed life-threatening, and so when she died, with me holding on to her in the bed, it just killed me. It was shocking. I wasn't ready. I was only in my forties, and I wasn't prepared for her to go. I wasn't willing to let her go.

After the viewing for my mother, I helped my dad get into the house, and he started to go too. We were by ourselves in my parents' home. I was alone with my dad as he pushed the oxygen tube away from his face and grasped for death. I straddled him on the bed, hugging him and pleading with all my energy and courage, inches from his face, "Dad, please don't go tonight. You cannot go!" I cried and begged him not to die.

"I just can't live without your mother," he said through his tears. All he wanted to do was go.

My dad didn't die that night, but six months later he took me into the bathroom, handed me his razor, and asked me to shave him for the last time. He stopped taking his medicine and took off his oxygen. I stayed with him, along with my siblings, and watched over him until he died later that day. In my heart, I wasn't willing to let my dad go either. I wasn't ready to handle being an orphan. Who would take my parents away from me within such a short time period? I get it. They were at an age to move on. It was good for them to go so quickly together. But I was young, I thought. Damn it! Hatred started to build within me.

Two years later, my sister Susan died of leukemia. She and I had been extremely close and connected on a lot of levels—like me, she was a banker and had blended a family. We could talk about anything together. We had the same views on civic policies, careers, family, beliefs, etc. We had common ground on pretty much everything. Losing her took a chunk out of my inner being. Hatred was beginning to peak. A couple years after that, my brother died too. After that, I was just generally pissed as hell, and I was done with deity. I was done with everything. I didn't voice that opinion very often, but if you got me going on the subject, you would have known it. Anger seeped from every pore.

Once, after my dad died, I tried to have a vision of him by drinking absinthe, a strong liquor that was rumored to be a hallucinogenic. Van Gogh used to drink it. I wanted to ask my dad why all these deaths were happening in our family. What was the point of it all? Why did Susan have to die the way she did? There are a lot of ways we try to explain away death—there's something "better" on the "other side;" it was so-and-so's "time"—but none of that made any sense to me. I had a lot of questions. Why take Susan away from her family? Wasn't she needed here too? I hate to be selfish, but I needed her here. And was it my brother's time? Was it really better on the other side? Is there really an "other side?"

Well, long story short, the vision didn't happen, and the absinthe made me sick as hell! Lesson learned. I'll never try that again.

But... when I woke up from my coma, all that hate was gone. Completely vanished. Dissolved. Instead, I was full of bliss, love, gratitude, and kindness. The thought of even having hate didn't come into my mind; the whole concept of hate was foreign to me. Later, when our kids teased me about my terrible behavior at Kootenai, or Laura told me stories of my misbehavior, it made me sick to my stomach. It was upsetting to me that my inner state and outer states weren't aligned. At IMC, I could have hugged anyone who came into my hospital room. I exuded love and peace and a certainty that everything was going to be okay. My friend David said it was as if I had a sort of eternal perspective on life. Worldly phenomenon seemed somewhat meaningless, and it was crystal clear to me that anything and everything would work out in the end because we are all internally connected.

When I was angry and hated God, I wanted answers. Now, I'm free of all that questioning. Though my blissed-out state faded over the course of a couple years and reality smacked me in the face full-force, I'm still grateful for the gift. There's a stark difference between the hate and anger I felt before, and the warmth and peace I feel now. I have no questions for God, or a higher power. I'm ready for whatever the next adventure is and I'm okay with not knowing what happens next and not having all the answers.

Given the near-death experience and my abrupt shift in brain orientation, I feel I've had a chance to live two lives within one lifetime. I'm grateful for that, because it's changed my perspective and enriched my capacity for emotional experiences.

From the word "go" I had a new focus on people, and it came very naturally to me to share personal, heart-to-heart things and encourage others to open up and do the same.

Out of curiosity, Laura had me retake the Myers–Briggs personality test. Before the accident, I was an ESTP (Extrovert, Sensing, Thinking, Perceiving), and after I was an INFP (Introvert, Intuiting, Feeling, Perceiving). Laura is an ENFP (Extrovert, Intuiting, Feeling, Perceiving). I'm definitely approaching life from a place of feeling rather than analysis. It just feels good to me now to focus on the emotional content of a situation, and to connect with people on a personal level. And while I was always on the cusp between extroversion and introversion, the brain injury pushed me more into the realm of introversion. This is somewhat typical for TBI survivors. We're more drawn to being alone. Many of us feel different and self-conscious around people. Many of us feel easily over stimulated by crowds, noise, and lights. You know I was definitely experiencing that. But for me, there was a positive twist: "Old Greg" may have been more extroverted, but just because I could work a room with confidence didn't mean I was connecting deeply with people. Back then, it just didn't come as easily to me. Now, I may be more reclusive, but when I do engage with people, it's more genuine and connected.

In general, many of my fellow survivors often don't relate well to others after brain injuries. We may feel that people just flat-out don't "get" us anymore. Brain injuries are known as an "invisible disease." Many of us who have them look fine from the outside, and everyone around us thinks we're okay. Many wonder what's the big deal with this person or that person who said they had serious problems. From the exterior, they look "perfectly normal." I can't tell you how many times I've heard that over the years.

There was one time, about six months after my accident, Laura and I went out to a local piano bar called the Tavernacle. I wasn't allowed to have alcohol for the first six months, so this was right after I'd gotten the authorization to drink. At this point, Laura was still pretty deep in the pit of post-traumatic stress. We were with Jimmy and a bunch of friends, all sitting around a big table. I could tell people were discussing me, but they were making a point to do it out of my earshot. They were whispering in each other's ears. My wits weren't completely there yet, but I could tell it was about me.

At one point in the evening, Laura became really sorrowful—big time, intensely sorrowful. She started crying and excused herself to the restroom. I was sitting there, kind of off to the side near a window, and I didn't know what to do. I didn't know exactly what was happening, but I knew that I was lost. Laura was having this fall-apart moment and I couldn't help her solve the problem or be a source of comfort like I typically would have. If I'd been in my usual frame of mind, I'd have taken control of the situation, gotten her away from the group and gone outside to take a walk or chat in the car for a bit.

It was always me and Laura. Whenever there was any sort of issue, I was her confidant. But because it was *about* me, I didn't know what to do. I was the problem. She was reaching out to others besides me, and I just sat there feeling sad and helpless and hoped that the other women there could comfort her. Whereas before I was a take-charge kind of guy, I found myself in a much more passive role and didn't know how to do it differently.

Later that evening, the group went back to Jimmy's condo for a party, and Laura and I were going to join. We all got in our cars and made our way over to Jimmy's, but when Laura and I pulled up to the curb of the towering condo building, we ended up just driving on. It seemed too overwhelming. There weren't any parking spots on the street, it was late at night, and my problem-solving capacity was shot. As we headed home, I tried to question Laura and figure out what exactly had been the problem at the bar. "Why was that such an intense moment? Were you sad about me? Were you mourning the loss of our relationship?" Laura replied, "D. All of the above."

Laura was still not accepting that the old Greg was gone; she kept thinking I was going to come all the way back, and the contrast was agonizing. She'd already fallen in love with me once, and accepted all of my quirks, and here I was asking her to do it all over again. It wasn't easy on her.

This scenario played itself out time and again over the course of years. Laura, mega extrovert that she is, craved the social life we used to have together. But I couldn't do it as often as she needed. I'd get overwhelmed and fatigued at parties and events, and my new introverted self just wanted to stay home anyway. We used to be active, fun-loving people with a wide and varied circle of friends. It was easy to form communities around the activities we did, like motorcycling, boating, and scuba diving. But those dropped away after the accident.

We stopped showing up and the relationships dried up; we could have made an effort, for sure, but Laura and I were both focused on much more pressing things. My relationships with my long-time friends seemed to be eroding. It was really hard on us both.

Laura and I had to make a conscious effort to cultivate new interests and connect with new people. Our new endeavors were more purpose-driven than adventure-driven. Laura joined a book group. She got into refurbishing furniture. I had my writing project. We both tried to get involved with the TBI community, but there wasn't much there for us. In the first half of 2012, Laura and I attended neuro rehab support groups at Intermountain Medical Center (IMC) and the University of Utah Hospital, but they were hit-or-miss.

When we first started at IMC, the monthly meetings were held at night in the basement of The Orthopedic Specialty Hospital (TOSH) in the physical therapy gym. At night, they'd pull out some chairs and set them up amidst the various pieces of exercise equipment and treatment tables. The group was small. Sometimes only four or five survivors would show up. It felt lonely and dark in half the room and the vibe wasn't dynamic. I was new and the topics didn't really fit me at first. There was nothing there for caregivers, so Laura wasn't getting anything out of it. I didn't meet any survivors who I could relate to out of the chute. I felt very alone in those early meetings.

The TBI support group at University Hospital was livelier. It was a larger group in a smaller, ground-floor space that had better lighting, and was attended by a whole mix of survivors. Some were immobilized. Others would blurt out inappropriate things at any given moment. Some were more in control or higher functioning. There was a whole range of people. By the time I started attending this particular group, I'd already been back at the bank for five or six months, and I was pretty high functioning. And it wasn't just my own self-perception. When I went to these groups, I could pick out the survivors. Even though TBI is thought of as an "invisible" problem, when I'm in a room with members of the community, I can pick out fellow survivors by their demeanor and how they hold their bodies.

When I started attending support groups, my cognitive ability was relatively good. I frequently got mistaken for a caregiver, not a survivor. I thought, "Holy cow, how could that be?" I'd just woken up from a coma a few months earlier, with the mindset of a young boy again. People see where I'm at now and some don't believe that my condition was as serious as it was. Sometimes there's disbelief. Sometimes there's judgment.

I always have to tell the story of my motorcycle accident, coma, and recovery before I can gain credibility. I tell them the gruesome details. That's because the way I speak, the way I write, the way I operate out in the world—I'm doing the seemingly impossible—relative to what I've been through. There are very few TBI survivors out there who are doing executive-level banking and writing books. It just doesn't happen often.

Six years after my accident, I asked Dr. Dodds how my recovery compared to other professionals (executives, lawyers, physicians, etc) who experienced a traumatic brain injury. He told me: "Greg, you are a freak." That made me laugh. "You're my only severe, check that, moderate or severe TBI patient to return to his previous professional position in the workforce in all my years of practicing medicine in this field." At that point, Dr. Dodds was only a few years from retirement, so he had a lot of years to draw on. While at first it made me laugh to hear Dr. Dodds describe me as a freak, his statement actually messed with me. I'd recovered more than most, and while I was grateful, I also felt undeserving. Being a freak, increased my experience of being undeserving, and increased my burden of debt. The same self-questioning arose: "Why me? Why not someone else?" But, that conversation didn't happen until six years after my TBI. Before that, I didn't know I was a freak. All I knew was that I was in limbo.

The TBI set us apart from our old activities and our old friends, and I wasn't quite fitting into the support groups I was attending. I continued to engage sporadically with the University Hospital group but Laura eventually stopped going altogether. There was nothing there for caregivers. That was a big theme of this whole ordeal: there was never anything there for the caregivers.

Later in that summer of 2012, about a year after my accident, Laura experienced another blow: Brianna, the office manager at Laura's business, passed away suddenly from a heroin overdose after being sober for years. Brianna had been Laura's rock in the aftermath of my accident. She'd taken on the burden of running Laura's business while Laura was taking care of me. And when Laura finally made it back to the office, Brianna had made a beach in the office, complete with sand, an umbrella, and beach chairs. She wanted Laura to feel some relaxation and joy. Brianna's sudden death was devastating to Laura. I share this story to highlight the fact that I wasn't even Laura's only problem. Life goes on, and my brain injury, plus her post-traumatic stress, just added an extreme level of difficulty to it.

Our lowest point happened one night in 2013, about two years after the accident. We'd gone out to dinner to an intimate little local restaurant with amazing food, and we'd had a great time. On the way home, we were driving down State Street, which is a busy road. It used to be the primary North-South road across Utah, and it's many lanes with lots of traffic. The moon was gorgeous that night, and Laura wanted to snap a quick picture of it. She wanted me to pause in the middle of the street to catch the shot. "Old" Greg would have pulled over in a heartbeat or stopped and put the hazard lights on. But I had traffic behind me—which always gets me to my worst anxiety. Plus, it was late in the day, which is when my cognitive functioning is at its worst. I just couldn't handle it.

"I need you to back up—I'm missing the picture," Laura said.

"I can't back up," I said. "We're on State Street. Let me take a left and turn around."

But Laura didn't want me to turn around. It was too late. She was annoyed that I wasn't living in the moment and wasn't daring enough to make a risky move like I would have back in the old days. I ended up just driving us straight home, and she was pissed by the time we walked through the door.

This situation, which seems like it should have been no big deal, was the match that lit the powder keg. Things blew up and exposed Laura's frustrations that had been building for a long time. We argued about everything. She was sick of feeling like everything in our life revolved around me. Her whole world had changed, our relationship was gone. The Greg she knew was gone. She felt like she'd sacrificed the last two years of her life. When I said "no" to pulling over to take that picture, she was understandably annoyed that she couldn't ask for even that one little thing. She didn't ask much of me—she knew my limits. But this was a breaking point. It just reminded her of every other time I had said "no" to her—of what we could no longer do, of how limited our social life had become because of how I'd changed. To me, the crux of the issue was that she wasn't able to accept the new reality of who I was. That had become obvious. And if she wasn't prepared to accept me for who I was, then we flat-out weren't going to make it.

And then, I said something that I would later regret forever. "Laura, this isn't just about you."

Looking back, that was just about the worst thing I could say to my caregiver, who'd been my rock through the worst days of the ordeal and who was obviously still struggling to process and move forward. My marriage to Laura is the number one most important thing in my life. But to her, I was dead and gone. The relationship we'd had was dead and gone. Meanwhile, her cares were going unnoticed. Everyone in our world was asking her, "How's Greg?" I can absolutely understand why, based on this reality, she and most other caregivers want to get the hell out. Caregivers are abandoned, lost, invisible. They deal with the most horrendous part of the TBI process and don't get the credit and support they need.

What I should have done in that moment, before opening my mouth and inserting my foot, was say, "Can we continue this conversation in the morning?" One of the most painful challenges I face after TBI is that I've lost some of my ability to problem-solve and maintain self-control when I'm faced with confrontation— and this happens especially late at night or when I'm fatigued. I don't behave well. I say really stupid things. Frankly, I'm shocked by what comes out of my mouth sometimes.

I'm generally very careful about how I say things; that's the true me. But when I'm fatigued or feel like I've been backed into a corner, I can lose my ability to control the way I phrase things, especially when it may be a difficult or emotionally weighty conversation. I'm known in my family for taking a long time to digest what somebody has said to me and to weigh my reply carefully so as not to amplify a problem situation.

Normally, I think through the ramifications of what I say and I completely own the fact that my words have consequences, especially in a large family where there can be a wide ripple effect. But when I'm exhausted and in the midst of a critical conversation, all that stuff goes right out the window. I just blurt out some crap that is the worst of me. It's not thoughtful. It's not measured. It makes me sound like an asshole. As I'm hearing myself say these kinds of things, and afterward when the words are hanging out on the airwaves, I think to myself, "Who the hell am I? I can't believe I just said that!"

It was ridiculous of me to say to Laura "it wasn't all about her." I completely own that. But at the time, I meant it. I was pissed.

With that, Laura said, "I just need to go away." She began to pack a bag and said she was going to stay at a hotel. "Maybe we just want different things."

Her words horrified me. Laura and I were married in 1994 and never once had we ever talked about divorce. And here she was ready to pack up and go. What had started as a stupid fight about a picture had, to my TBI mind, turned into the potential dissolution of the relationship that meant the world to me, with my best friend, my lover, my partner. I started crying and begged her not to go.

"You're the only thing I want," I said. "There's nothing in this life that's more important to me than you." But sometimes, in a hard moment, there's no going back. Sometimes you can't say sorry enough for the words you say. There's not enough apologies. Not enough hugs. The damage was done.

Laura didn't end up leaving that night, but she took a pillow and blanket and went to sleep on the couch. At that point, we'd been married for almost two decades and I could count on one hand how many times we'd gotten to that place of disconnect, with one of us on the damn couch. I stayed in our bedroom, thinking things were coming to an end and that I was on the precipice of losing everything. I knew that if I lost her, I'd lose everything that was important to me. I went through awakening moments after my coma and had my priorities in order: keep my marriage and family together; relearn how to speak, read, write, and walk; and get my job back. I just couldn't figure out how not stopping to take a photo of the moon could escalate to the breakup of our marriage. But I've found that one of the many side effects of traumatic brain injury is that seemingly banal arguments can take on new and bigger meaning...

Our marriage didn't end that day—or any other day, thankfully. I don't know how Laura went about deciding that she wanted to stay together, but she didn't go anywhere, and things gradually started getting better over time. We wake up every day and decide we want to be married. Marriage isn't easy in general, and we've faced some out-of-the-ordinary challenges. It's not easy pulling together a blended family. It's not easy managing a TBI. We work through things and then we move on. We work our butts off to be married, and the thing that keeps us together is that we're best friends. It is the basis of us. Truly best friends. That's what we hold on to.

21

As I've mentioned, when I was first released from IMC in September of 2011, Laura set up a rehab and rest area for me in our living room. Our couch was the central point, and I unknowingly took ownership of it. Our living room became the headquarters for my therapy, napping, and television watching. My "man cave." I have fond memories of that comfy Stickley leather couch. It symbolized the improvements I made. But it was the opposite for Laura. She started to view the couch as the center of a rehab process that may never end, as well as a symbol of the long-term changes that she hadn't asked for and didn't want.

When, after many months, I finally understood the impact this was having on her, I gave the couch back to Laura. In other words, I stopped using it. It was my way of showing her that we were going to be okay despite the fact that we were on a new path. Laura covered the couch with new throw pillows and hoped the memories would go away. But that wasn't enough.

Laura says that when I became obsessed with researching and writing about my accident in 2012, I gained a sense of purpose after being lost. I was less needy and had a project to focus on, and that lifted a weight from her shoulders and gave her some freedom. She didn't have to constantly worry about me and could focus on her own needs. We had become more homebound than we were accustomed to being, but she could sense that I could start taking care of myself. So, Laura was able to find a new hobby. She and her friends started refurbishing old furniture. They'd find old wooden pieces and refinish them in a "shabby chic" style. I have fond (if hazy) memories of sitting out on our deck with rock music playing over the sound system, Laura working on her furniture with friends, me writing my book. It gave Laura a feeling of relief to be able to be creative. She could breathe again.

In 2013, Laura decided we needed to redecorate the house. She just couldn't stand it anymore. The dark, heavy furniture—and especially my beloved couch—all reminded her of the past, and of what we'd lost. We sold all that incredible Stickley furniture for a song. It killed me, but Laura needed to get it out of the house. She replaced it all. The new couches and armchairs were in lighter fabrics with a variety of prints and colors and textures. We had a bunch of shabby chic tables and chairs, plus handcrafted decorations that Laura made. She did some painting. The place was bright, colorful, and cheery. Before, when Laura wanted something new for the house, she'd head over to Pottery Barn and buy it. Now she made it or refurbished something herself. The few pieces she purchased fit perfectly with the furniture she made herself. It was a whole new style to signal a new period in our life. And a whole new hands-on attitude. Taking control of her outer world helped Laura take control of her inner world. No more "off the shelf" living for us. We had to make our own life.

* * *

In the spring of 2013, Laura and I attended a three-day Franklin Covey conference for TBI couples that was put on by the Brain Injury Alliance of Utah. The program was really good from what I remember, but, for Laura, this was a watershed moment. At one point in the weekend, the TBI survivors and their caregivers were separated into two groups, and for the first time, Laura was able to connect with other caregivers. They talked openly about their struggles and issues, out of earshot of us survivors. These were people who could truly empathize with what Laura was going through. She was blown away. That experience changed everything for her. She came away from that weekend inspired to develop a support group for TBI caregivers. It was the foundation of what would become the first of its kind in Utah. Finally, Laura's independence and drive could work in her favor.

It just so happened that shortly before that conference, Laura and I had met with Larry Hancock, CEO of the Urban Central Region of Intermountain Healthcare (the parent company of Intermountain Medical Center). We'd requested a meeting with Larry to thank him for all that IMC's Neuro Rehab Specialty Group had done to help me recover and for the support they gave to our family. This was at the time when I was handing out bound copies of "Warmth and a Bad Fish," and so I gave him one with a handwritten note on the cover and signed it.

LeeAnne, the EVP from my bank, sat on Larry's board, and he was helpful in my transfer from Kootenai Health. He was kind and amazingly tender with us, asking about our family and the physicians and therapists who'd helped me recover. Toward the end of our meeting, he asked, "What can I do for you?" That shocked Laura and me, and we didn't know what to say. We were there to thank him, not ask anything of him. At the time, I just reiterated my gratitude, stumbling over my words in surprise.

But, later, when Laura had her "ah-ha!" moment about starting a TBI caregiver support group, she decided to take Larry up on his offer—and he came through. Larry provided Laura with a conference room in Building 1 (the administrative tower) of the IMC complex. Her brain injury caregiver group would have a space to call home.

It's not an understatement to say that starting Utah's first TBI caregiver support group changed Laura's world. She says, "Caregivers leave the hospital with their toolbox pretty much empty; I had to earn my hammer, saw, and screwdriver the hard way." Starting the group was both a survival mechanism for herself as well as a way to create a supportive community. She needed to be around her peers and be able to talk openly with people who could relate. And it became clear from the get-go that other caregivers were craving the same thing. The turnout was huge. Caregivers drove in from all over the place to attend the meetings. Soon word-of-mouth spread and attendees arrived from surrounding counties. There were so many people, the group spent the first few meetings just introducing themselves and getting to know each other.

The group included caregivers across the spectrum. Some had a survivor who was still in the neuro rehab unit in the adjacent hospital, and some had been caregiving for decades. For a while after the start of the group, people just wanted to talk, and the meetings were informal. People would share tips and offer support to members who were feeling hopeless or depressed. A licensed clinical social worker, or therapist was on hand to support those who were in deep trauma.

But after a while, the focus of the group shifted. Laura wanted to be sure that people walked away with something tangible. It's hard for caregivers to take time for themselves, and she wanted to help them make the most of that time. So, while sometimes the group did "open mic" sessions and gave people the opportunity to have their stories be heard, more often they had an educational aspect, that included guest speakers with an expertise in a particular topic. They would share practical information relevant to taking care of survivors—dealing with insurance, finding resources, and so on—but a big focus was on helping caregivers best take care of themselves. They would talk about maintaining hope, persevering in the face of struggles, grieving their losses, adjusting to life as a caregiver, finding their "village" to rely upon—all things that their fellow TBI caregivers could truly relate to, and which they could discuss, without fear of judgment, in a supportive environment. "At the end of the day, just having fellow caregivers to talk to meant everything," Laura says.

It felt unbelievably good to Laura to help people do what she floundered to do herself when she first started caregiving for me. She didn't want people to feel as lost and depressed as she did at the beginning. Laura's involvement with caregivers also gave her new perspective on our situation. She heard from caregivers whose survivors were in extreme situations. Some had survivors who were physically immobile and were navigating life in a wheelchair or couldn't get out of bed. Others were caring for survivors who'd completely lost their ability to communicate or had radical personality changes that left them mean, angry, or unpredictable. Still others were unmotivated in their rehab, or had "given up," which left their caregivers deeply frustrated. Relative to so many other people, Laura and I were exceedingly lucky, and we were grateful for that and for the continued strength of our partnership.

Being around her fellow caregivers was the source of healing Laura needed, while also allowing her to pay it forward by providing a safe place for other caregivers. Gradually, over the course of years, the post-traumatic stress lost its grip on her and she felt healed.

22

Connecting with caregivers and creating a supportive network was a huge game-changer for Laura. I likewise felt the urge to give back in a meaningful way. Before the accident, I'd done plenty of volunteer work. The bank I worked for encouraged us to contribute to the community, so I'd sit on charity boards and volunteer at events.

I loved volunteering at the Children's Center once a week and reading books to underprivileged kids during my lunch hour. Those were feel-good moments that couldn't be duplicated. On large, influential committees, I would help run and fundraise for an annual black-tie gala. We'd spent months planning it and would raise a hundred grand and feel really good about it. But it was also a part of my job. I definitely wouldn't have wanted to volunteer in a hospital. Medical environments have always made me queasy.

But after the accident, I felt an urgent need to give back to the brain injury community. It went beyond just a need. I was driven. It was an unspoken desire from somewhere within. I felt a huge burden of debt because I felt like I'd been given gifts that I hadn't done anything to deserve. Dr. Dodds said this was normal. From a neuropsychological standpoint, anybody who is given something that they feel they don't deserve, medically, has to come to terms with it somehow. Of course, there are some entitled people out there who have a big ego and think everything is theirs to take. But if you're a normal guy or gal and have some humility, it can be easy to feel guilty. "Survivors' Guilt" is a psychological term that describes feelings of unworthiness or guilt in those who survive traumatic events, or when a survivor experiences feelings of guilt because they somehow, miraculously reach full recovery when others don't. There aren't many people who reach the kind of recovery levels I have, and I kept asking myself, "Why me?" I still don't understand why.

I had been given the ability to empathize and connect with people in an incredible way, and I felt like I had to make use of it. Otherwise, why were those gifts given to me? I'm just a guy. I haven't done anything special in my life. Who am I? Honestly. I'm just a Regular Joe who grew up on the poor side of town and made tons of mistakes in my life. I don't deserve what I've been given. I focused on myself for most of my life. I was a career-driven and materialistic man, and I had a lot of success in that. I was a good guy, a good husband, and a good blended-family dad, but so are a ton of others. There are lots of decent people out there. Why was it that I survived three TBIs and a coma and came away with incredible gifts, while some other guy slips and falls on ice in a parking lot, hits the back of his head once and dies? Why do I get to have all the cognitive capacity that I do, while some other guy who crashed his motorcycle will never be able to speak again, or work again, or remember who he is from to day to day? Why do I have what I have?

* * *

In January of 2013, Dr. Dodds finally gave me permission to start volunteering with the outpatient neuro rehab team at TOSH—the same team that helped me after I was released from IMC. It was an intense three-month process to get final approval as an official volunteer. So, about a year and a half after my accident, I was good to go. I met with Heather, the volunteer coordinator, after Dr. Dodds gave me the go-ahead to start volunteering.

Heather, like most folks who meet me for the first time, wanted to know everything about my accident, coma, and recovery experience. She was incredibly sweet and teared up as I told her my story. Then she guided me through every step of the application process. It was like applying for a job. I had to submit a resume and reference letters, get a full-on background check, pass a complete medical exam, and go through a four-week round of immunizations and shots. Once I passed all that, I had to do trainings in classrooms and online. Holy crap, it was a lot. And remember, I was working my full-time banking job, keeping my marriage together, and writing a book.

Heather was totally in my corner. An amazing advocate. She saw that I wasn't a typical volunteer. Most hospital and medical center volunteers have more general roles. They sacrifice, work hard and graciously volunteer their time and energy in gift shops and help out at Help stations in waiting areas or drive golf carts to transport patients and caregivers. I didn't fit the typical volunteer mold. Very few volunteers are specifically assigned to a unit with a specific skill set or mentoring experience. I specifically wanted to work with my fellow TBI survivors and their caregivers. That's what I was passionate about. Heather caught on to that very quickly and helped her boss understand my unique situation. They accepted me into their amazing volunteer family.

Dr. Dodds hooked me up for volunteer work with Kim, my outpatient speech therapist. Kim immediately had me join her aphasia group, which met twice a week for an hour during lunch in the conference room at IMC's outpatient neuro rehab at Tosh, my second home after my accident.

I'll never forget my first day. I had no idea this particular aphasia support group even existed, but I would have done anything Kim asked me to do, anytime she asked me to do it. I felt like I owed her so much. So, even though I didn't know exactly what it meant to volunteer for the aphasia group, I said "yes" without hesitation. I didn't really know what I was doing there, but I was happy to be there doing it. When I walked in on day one, sitting around the table were brain injury survivors like me, but Kim and I were the only ones with IHC badges hanging from lanyards around our necks. Kim said, "I'd like to introduce Greg, our newest aphasia group member and volunteer." Kim asked me to tell everyone about myself, so I mumbled that I was a former patient of Kim's and had recovered from a Harley accident and was hopeful I could help. Lame! But Kim and the group welcomed me warmly. As everyone introduced themselves, I discovered that the survivors were primarily stroke patients who had difficulty with speech impediments. Saying even just a couple words was hard for some of them.

After we were done playing a game, I knew who the core, longstanding members of the group were. After the group session, they each hugged me and made me feel like a million bucks for joining their special world. I was accepted immediately as a fellow survivor, even though most of them had suffered strokes and I was a dumbass adrenaline junkie who'd wrapped his head around too many poles. TBI survivors and stroke survivors with aphasia are usually fighting similar but different battles, and for whatever reason, over the years of volunteering I've seen that it's the stroke survivors who seem to hang on in our group longer than my fellow TBI buddies.

I'm a bit of an odd duck in that regard. But they were warm and inviting and cared for me. It felt great. I felt accepted. These folks really showed that they needed me, wanted me, and appreciated my presence. They were endeared to me, and vice versa. I was technically volunteering for them, but Kim and the aphasia group members were watching out for me too. They became an extension of my neuro rehab, and I received much more than I gave.

* * *

As soon as I started volunteering with the aphasia group, I immediately wanted to give back with inpatient survivors on the twelfth floor at Intermountain Medical Center's Neuro Rehab Specialty Group—where I had my first memory. These are the folks who've just had their injury or stroke or whatever it was that brought them to the hospital, and they're in their earliest stages of recovery, oftentimes just out of the ICU. The administrators wouldn't allow me to volunteer on the twelfth floor, but it probably won't surprise you to hear that I kept asking. I asked about it probably as much as I asked for some Advil during those early days.

In 2015, I came across an article in the *Wall Street Journal*, titled "Mentors Help Patients with Rehab and Offer Insider Tips Along the Way," by Laura Landro. It was about hospitals across the country that were using former patients as mentors. This was exactly what I wanted to do at IMC, and it inspired me to propose a mentoring program of my own. Who better to mentor someone in crisis than a former patient who'd been there before? I wanted to become a mentor manager, bringing in former patients and training them to become mentors in specific specialties. So, I set up a meeting with Brad Zollinger, who was the Director of the Neurosciences Institute at IMC. It just so happened that Brad's office was on the twelfth floor and he knew me from watching my rehab.

Using the *Wall Street Journal* article as my starting point, I researched how to set up and run mentoring programs. After preparing a business plan and a well-thought-out strategic integration plan, including the *Journal* article, I had a full-on thirty-page packet ready for Brad and his administrators. I called upon my Banker Bob ways to present the proposal. After I handed out the packet, as if I were in Senior Loan Committee, Brad kindly let me talk for about ten minutes before cutting me off. He'd heard enough. He said, "Greg thank you for going through the effort of putting this proposal together, but there's no way I'm going to back a mentor program for the entire hospital." He went on to say, "I just want you to be a mentor on our team—to be a member of our medical team." Brad said the words I'd actually been wanting to hear—Wow! I almost jumped out of my chair and hugged him, but I kept myself composed. I expressed how much I appreciated his confidence in me.

From that day forward, I had permission from Brad to shadow medical professionals on the floor. He sent out an email notifying the entire department, and he assigned someone to coordinate my training and help identify appropriate patients and caregivers for me to connect with.

I was on cloud nine. Totally euphoric. This was a years-long goal of mine, and finally I'd get to realize it. I was immensely satisfied in a way I'd never experienced before. My whole life, everything I'd accomplished was for the sake of materialism and moving up the ranks within my career and making more and more money and gaining more and more prestige. This gift that Brad had given me, this opportunity, had nothing to do with money or prestige or title or anything that I was used to seeking. Brad gave me something better—an opportunity to give back to the community that had given so much to me at IMC. I would have the opportunity to further balance the debt I felt I owed for the gifts I'd been given, directly to inpatient survivors and caregivers on the very floor where I received rehab tools I still use today.

On another level, Brad's go-ahead was a compliment to me and my recovery. After trying for years, I'd finally reached a level of cognitive capacity where I could present my ideas in a persuasive way in the medical community. It was immensely meaningful to me that he trusted me to mentor in the most critical setting in the neuro rehab world and to help people during the most sensitive moments of their lives. I was on a high of satisfaction. Thinking about it brings tears to my eyes to this day, to know that he felt I could use my experience to help others overcome their hurdles. The same obstacles I overcame. Some I'm still battling today.

Before he let me loose on the twelfth floor, Brad made me give him a promise. He said, "Greg, having you walk down the hallways, without you even saying a word, might give patients false hope. So you have to promise me that you will be careful not to give patients false hope as a mentor." With that, he sat quietly and waited for me to answer. There was an awkward silence. He was flat-out serious. This was the biggest risk in him giving me authority to be a mentor. After the silence, I promised him. I would do my best to avoid giving patients false hope. Of course, what is false hope, exactly? What's the line between real hope and false hope? It's not black and white. To this day I'm not sure I can truly distinguish the two, but I took the promise to heart.

Every time I walk into IMC as a volunteer, my goal is to create feel-good moments with people who desperately need them. These moments take place in the acute wing of the hospital, in a diversity of situations—they're in a hospital bed, in the clinic gym, walking through the halls. Sometimes the person has had an injury or a stroke or they've tried to harm themselves. Sometimes it's a conversation with a caregiver, or with just a survivor, or with both. No two brain injuries are alike. As the saying goes, if you've seen one brain injury, you've seen one brain injury.

There's no such thing as a "typical" day for me as a volunteer, because I honestly never know what I'm going to run into. But usually, when I arrive at IMC, first I'll go to the speech therapist to see if they have survivors they'd like me to spend time with. Then I'll go to the gym and see who's in there and sit with people who are doing puzzles or games, or people doing physical therapy. I just start chatting. People don't know who I am and they're wondering what I'm doing there, because I look like a therapist with a badge or Normal Joe. At some point, I'm introduced as a former patient. Often one of the medical personnel will say, "Greg is a TBI survivor who now volunteers and mentors on our floor." If I introduce myself, I always point out the room I was in. Room 1219. And I have an instant connection with whoever I'm talking to. The response is always immediate curiosity, and then the questions start. What happened? How long ago? What were your injuries? Did you have aphasia? You look great, but do you have any problems? Are you fully recovered? How long did it take? How did you recover so well?

Survivors and caregivers always ask me how long it took to recover. That's one of those questions I have to jump around, depending on who the person is. For one thing, I don't want to offer anything that could be perceived as false hope. And for another, I don't feel like I *have* recovered completely. Definitely not fully. I still have issues that I work on every day. I let people know that I still battle fatigue daily, and that I struggle to convert short-term memory to long-term. I have issues with depression, mood swings, and rumination. I tend to be reclusive like most survivors. I still have aphasia issues, especially at night when I'm fatigued. I'm good at dancing around word-finding problems. I tell survivors that I use the tools—the ones they're being given *right now*—years later, for myself. They're in awe. They ask, "For real?" To them—and to most people—I might look like I'm fully recovered, but I say "guess again," because I have issues that I'm still working on.

I feel really good about my recovery, and I've worked my butt off, but I'm still working and will continue to develop my brain throughout my lifetime using the same neuro rehab tools they have in their hands. I tell fellow survivors, "I want you to reach out and hug your therapist and thank them for the tools they're giving you right now." It's an awe-inspiring moment of love and warmth. Lots of hugs all around. And I feel like I get to inspire some hope without breaking my promise to Brad. I just tell people about what happened to me and what I've done to recover, and I ask what I can do to help them.

Of course, people are at all sorts of cognitive levels, and I meet people where they're at in terms of understanding what they're trying to express to me. Sometimes folks are embarrassed because they have disinhibition and say something inappropriate—but I was there too and it doesn't bother me for a second. Sometimes they're frustrated with their communication ability and can't get their words out. I remember those feelings. Sometimes they can only speak a few words, or they have serious aphasia, and I wait patiently for them to get their words out. At times, I interpret their hand and eye signals or wait for them to write something out on a piece of paper.

Or, if their caregiver is there, they can help me figure out what the survivor is trying to say. Either way, we relate to each other because I've been there, done that. All of us survivors have each other's backs. The worst thing we can do as survivors is compare ourselves to anyone but ourselves. That's nuero rehab 101 that I remember being reinforced early on in room 1219. Therapists only showed me my results and chatted about my progress. We *never* discussed any other patients on the floor. Why would we?

I do have a memory of being in the gym and getting excited for the survivor next to me who was taking her first step. We all celebrated the hell out of that moment!

The takeaway? We can only track our own development. If someone else has a good moment, sure, be a cheerleader! But if we stall, and it happens to all of us in the brain injury survivor world, then we can lean on each other and our caregivers, take a "brain break," and get back up. As the famous street artist Banksy wrote on one of his pieces, a painting of a little girl and a blue bird: "If you get tired, learn to rest, not quit."

Sometimes I'll have one-on-one time with a caregiver as a mentor and do my best to answer their questions. Just being with brain injury caregivers is extremely important to me. Whatever is needed in the moment, I let the conversation move organically. I know that caregivers are overwrought and trying to keep it together. Back in the day when I was on the twelfth floor as a patient, like their survivors, I didn't fully comprehend where I was, what was going on, or what it all meant. But Laura did, and she was going through agony. As my caregiver in those early days, Laura had the burden of understanding the global ramifications of the accident while I was focused on putting a butterfly puzzle together. The survivor is micro-oriented, while the caregiver has a full view of the global fallout. They're feeling the weight of the world crushing down on them. So, depending on the situation, sometimes those one-on-one conversations with caregivers are unbelievably heartfelt and critical as I mentor their survivors.

The first couple I mentored was a survivor, who had aphasia, and their spouse. I remember having a long conversation with them in the hospital room. The survivor was in bed and their spouse sat in a chair next to me. I was just sharing my usual spiel—that I'd been a patient there myself in room 1219, what Laura had done to save my life. I told them about putting my butterfly puzzle together and how Laura got me an iPad. I shared some humorous moments along with the hard moments. I asked the survivor's recovery status and gave encouragement to take advantage of the rehab tools the therapists were teaching. But the whole time, as I was talking, the mechanics of the whole survivor thing seemed secondary. It seemed like the easy part.

The harder part was that while I was talking, I was cognizant of the spouse's distress. At one point during this conversation, I gently put my hand on their arm as I continued to chat with the survivor, and I felt like I was able to confer some calm to the spouse without breaking the conversation with the survivor. They asked me about my relationship with Laura, and about how we made it.

I don't remember the words that we spoke, but I remember the feeling of them looking at each other tenderly as I told them what Laura had gone through to care for me. I said to the survivor, "Please let your partner know how much you appreciate all the care given to you each day. Acknowledge how hard it is for your caregiver to go through this with and for you. Say 'thank you' as often as you possibly can."

This was my first experience as a mentor, and it was beautiful. I felt like I bonded with these two immediately, and their love for each other was so strong and apparent, and I loved them as soon as I met them. They just hugged me and couldn't stop. Two days later I happened to meet them outside the entryway to the hospital, sitting on the edge of the fountain. "Greg!" they called out. And then they came up to me and sandwiched me in a great big bear hug.

Another time, I had a heartwarming one-on-one with a survivor who was in a state of hopelessness and despair when we first met. We were immediately internally connected and I could sense complete loss. I don't remember much about the injuries or the particulars of the situation—or really, of most patients I work with. The details aren't important. What matters are the emotions of the moment.

In this case, the survivor had little self-esteem. They were utterly demoralized. I sensed that this survivor's doom and negativity were severe. When people wake up in the hospital with a TBI and realize their whole world has changed and the impact it's had on their loved ones, some think it would have been better for everybody if they hadn't survived. I admit, in my lowest moments, thoughts like this have crossed my mind. They think their loved ones would have an easier time getting over their death than dealing with the continual ramifications of living with a TBI survivor, and the constant reminder that their life would never be the same again. I can sense it when people are in that dark place because I've been there. But I just stayed with the survivor and continued to connect on an even deeper level the more we talked. It's one of the gifts I was given in my coma. I have an innate ability to connect with others internally at times, if they're receptive.

We cried and talked about how the rehab tools given by the therapists would work—*if* the survivor made the choice to accept them. They had the power to use those tools, if they chose, to recover at the highest level possible for them. And their loved ones would support and embrace them. A couple days later, the survivor told their family about our connection and they found me in the gym. They came over and hugged me. It felt amazing. What made this memorable was that the survivor shared our connection with family members, and the emotion of the moment transitioned from doom to joy. They understood.

I get referrals to TBI survivors from the community. One of these referrals was for a survivor who had attempted suicide. These are really tough moments. Initially, I didn't know what to do or say, but the survivor was open about what they'd attempted, and they appreciated my help. I thought it would be different than a person who'd been injured in an accident or had a stroke, but we connected in the same way as I would with any other survivor. The questions and concerns were the same. We continued to work together much longer than I expected that day, and we bonded. The survivor's caregivers were so grateful for our time spent with each other, and when I left, the survivor told me they were on a new and healthy path.

Volunteering with TBI survivors and caregivers, being there to offer some comfort and connection and perspective in a critical time of their lives, it was everything I'd hoped it would be and more.

23

Now, if this were a Hollywood movie, it would have ended with the last chapter. I got my job back—yay! Laura started a caregiver group—whoo-hoo! Our relationship remained strong and our family was growing thanks to the addition of our children's spouses and new babies. We were giving back to the TBI community, Laura had healed from post-traumatic stress, and I'd reached an incredible level of recovery after my injury. It's all good! Fade to black as we ride off into the sunset.

But, as you know, this is real life, and things don't tie up that neatly.

We did return to a place of relative normalcy, Laura and I. For a few years, we were both working, the mortgage was getting paid, we were fulfilled by our volunteer work, and we found new ways to indulge the adventurous spirit that had kept us bonded as a couple for more than twenty years. As our marriage counselor had told us in 1994 when we were embarking on blending our families, it was important for us to make time for ourselves as a couple, just the two of us, as often as possible. Adventures cemented our relationship in the past, and after my accident we kept the spirit and modified the details. We've had getaways to Mexico and New York City, and Laura even bought me a flying lesson for my birthday one year. I'd always entertained a dream of being a pilot, but I'd never taken an actual lesson. It was a flat-out blast, though I knew I'd be "one and done" because getting a pilot's license is a big (and expensive) undertaking. But taking one lesson was right in my wheelhouse, and it gave me a kick after I'd hung up my adrenaline-rush "spurs" years earlier, as my neurosurgeon and others had begged me to do after surviving three traumatic brain injuries.

Things were going well—until circumstances sent us crashing into a ditch of a different sort.

I'd served as the director of commercial lending for my region at the bank for fifteen years. It was a job I was asked to create back in 1999, and it was replicated in other regions throughout all of Utah and Idaho. I loved it. I'd been offered various promotions over the years that allowed me this opportunity. I had also been offered bank president positions at small community banks, but I'd turned them all down. But then, in 2014, my department shifted—my bank partner Brad was promoted, the Salt Lake region was split in two, my team was in flux. So when, in 2015, I was offered a promotion to a sales management position, it seemed like it was finally time to make a jump. It was a decision I'd later regret.

* * *

Changes were afoot at the bank. It was announced that we were in the process of cutting millions in expenses because of turmoil in the financial sector. And those of us in senior management knew that, once cost cuts had been achieved by streamlining systems and centralizing operations, the Bancorp would move on to cutting labor. We were bankers; we could do the math. Things began to happen quickly, and the ax eventually made its way to other senior positions such as mine. Since I'd taken that promotion, I didn't have my commercial lending team under me anymore. It was a sales-only position, with no direct reports. It was expendable. Over the course of the year since the initial announcement, I saw folks around me being let go. Positions were being cut weekly—and these were people at my level. Everyone, myself included, was wondering when they were going to get that proverbial tap on the shoulder.

In January 2016, I heard the words, "Greg, your job has been eliminated." I shouldn't have been shocked, given all the layoffs happening around me, but those words... they just about broke me. I couldn't allow the words to fully penetrate. I had to block them at that very moment or I just would have lost it. A protective mechanism kicked in. I couldn't allow myself to feel the full force of it. The conversation had a surreal quality, almost like it wasn't really happening or I was hearing it as a third party. I was listening to the sound coming at me but struggling to believe it. It couldn't be happening. I'd been doing this work for thirty-five-plus years. It was all I knew. I couldn't fathom the implications of *not* being a banker anymore. The idea of it was impossible. It hurt beyond measure, but I'd put in my dues. I was very grateful that I was offered a full year's severance package.

It was one of the toughest days of my life. As a finance guy, I got it—I knew, from a financial perspective, the cuts were unavoidable. But I didn't just lose a job that day. I lost family. I lost my identity. I lost a place filled with memories. The bank had been my focus twenty-four hours a day, seven days a week. I never clocked out—never wanted to. I had my phone with me all the time, and I made myself available any time to answer my team's questions and help them make deals. I was endlessly driven to make myself successful and make my team successful.

The bank was also where I'd met some of my best friends—including Laura. She worked at the bank back when she was a single mother supporting three kids. At the time, I was a commercial lender and was working hard to prove myself and stand out among the many lenders at the head office. Laura and I both had very strong work ethics and did whatever it took to excel. This was back when the bank was smaller, and we had a core inner circle of friends who worked on the same floor, which also included the offices of the CEO, president, director of commercial lending, the senior loan committee, as well as the board room. During the eighties and nineties, every major decision that drove the bank's growth and success happened on that floor around us. We were the epicenter. Our individual successes actually resulted in increasing the stock price of the bank. If I booked a multimillion dollar deal, it resulted in improving the stock price of the bank back in those days. Pretty heady stuff.

I was very proud to say I was a banker. I couldn't imagine not saying that. It's part of who I was and was all I'd ever known, starting when I was a kid at age seventeen, working my way up the ladder. I declined opportunities to serve as president at other local banks because I was so invested in the company. It was expected that I would be one of the few handpicked to run the bank as others left. I was known as a "lifer," in both the positive and negative sense of the word.

Even though I was devastated to leave, I didn't think for a second that I'd have trouble finding something else. I was well-connected and had direct access to the executive-level decision makers at every bank in the area. Laura and I thought, "No problem. I'll have a new job in two weeks, a month tops." I interviewed with every national and local bank. I was going on four to six interviews a week. Some days I had two or three stacked up. I met with everybody. And I got nowhere. Not a single job offer. All I was hearing at all of these banks is that they were in the same situation that my former bank was in—either they were laying off senior management people, or they had a hiring freeze, or both. They were cutting costs. I even widened the net and started looking for work in the medical world, since I was loving the work I was doing in a volunteer capacity. I reached out of my comfort zone and looked for management positions within IHC and within health insurance companies since I once had my insurance license.

After six months and fifty interviews—yes, *fifty*—and still no job, Laura and I were floored. What the hell was going on? We had to wonder if it was because of the TBIs. Word was getting around, despite all the work that Laura and I'd done to keep the worst of the details on lockdown and present me to the world as a put-together guy. I certainly didn't mention it to prospective employers. But even those who didn't know about the TBIs would find out immediately if they Googled me, since there were multiple articles and videos online from various news outlets.

An in-depth story about the crash and its aftermath had been featured in *Catalyst* magazine and was available online. There was an ABC news report about the accident, plus information about speaking events I'd done at IMC and at the University of Utah. But nobody had cause to Google me until I was job-searching after the layoff in February 2016. Before, I was being offered bank president positions, and after February 2016 I couldn't get even a commercial lending position or a team leader position. One bank toyed with the idea of hiring me as a Small Business Association specialist, but that position was a hundred levels below where I'd been at the bank, and I wasn't even the right person for it.

A question nagged at me: Were prospective employers discounting me because of the TBI, even after the herculean effort I'd made to recover to such an incredible extent?

Eventually, I determined that I was unemployable. Even beyond the TBI, I had other factors going against me—mainly my age and the level of seniority I'd achieved. Positions like mine weren't being replaced; they were being eliminated. And the people who were being hired were younger people who were willing to work for less. I got no's all over the place, from people I knew and respected. After six months, I walked away from the experience thinking, "I am nothing. I am nobody anymore." My ego was completely deflated. I couldn't have been any lower.

The ending of my banking career was a huge loss to me on all levels—financially, emotionally, and to my sense of who I was as a person. Banking was part of my identity. Even now, years after the layoff, I still say "I'm a banker." It just slips out. It probably always will. People still ask me banking questions and for banking advice. When I'm in an environment with other bankers, I still say "we" as if I'm still at the bank. "If you come to *us*, *we*'ll help you do x, y, or z."

Circumstances sent me spiraling into a depression. I was lost. I reached an even lower point than I did after the accident, if you can believe it. At least, when I'd had the accident, I had my bliss state to buffer me from the harsh realities of my situation. Everything seemed possible through those rose-colored lenses. Yes, there'd been a grieving process in the aftermath of the TBI, but the grieving process I went through after losing my banking career felt even worse. Emotionally, I was struggling to keep one nostril above water. For a while, I could barely drag myself off the couch, and I didn't leave the house except to attend neuro psychology sessions.

There was also the fact that my job loss threw our future into a new level of uncertainty. Laura and I had worked incredibly hard for decades; we'd paid our dues and were looking forward to being able to take a break and enjoy the fruits of our labor. This derailment of my career threw all those plans out the window. We went from feeling financially secure to wondering where the next mortgage payment was going to come from.

I needed to find a new pathway.

24

You may have figured out by now that even when I get knocked down, I'm not the kind of person to stay down. And so, while I was grieving the loss of my career, it wasn't long before I picked up my head to look around and find a new direction. I needed to find a path in life, and it had to be based on what was motivating me in my career *now*. I used to get a high from doing million-dollar loans for corporations. I used to be motivated by money and prestige. But now I get that high from connecting with people and inspiring them. I wanted to find something that would allow me to do that.

As is true with so much of life, serendipity had a role to play. In 2012, just a little over a year from when I had my accident, I was invited to speak at an anniversary celebration dinner being held by IMC's neuro rehabilitation team. Of course, I had to say yes to the team that had changed my life. The room was filled with a couple hundred or more members of the department, including executives, physicians, therapists, psychologists, nurses, and spouses. When it was my turn at the podium, I did a "show and tell" of some of the items that meant a lot to me during my early recovery, like my iPad, my black binder, and my Frosted Flakes—which I immediately spilled all over the podium. That got a good laugh.

Then I led them through my recovery experience, from my awakening moment to relearning how to speak, read, write, and walk again, thanks to the critical tools that had been given to me by the medical professionals in that room. Tears were flowing from me and from audience members. I didn't realize it at the time, but I'd just delivered my first inspirational keynote address, to the team that had brought me back to reality.

Over the years, I had other opportunities to speak about my experience. In May 2013, Laura and I gave a presentation to the University of Utah Hospital TBI support group. This was one of the things I did to pay back the burden of debt that I felt weighed heavily on my shoulders. The more support group sessions I attended, the more I realized the ways I stood out among my fellow survivors, even though I was still facing daily challenges with fatigue and memory issues. I saw that I'd received gifts that were uncommon—like my newfound ability to empathize and quickly create meaningful connections with people. Sharing my experience in the group environment was a way to give back and share my gifts. Laura and I spoke together to the survivors and caregivers, sharing a message of hope and encouraging them to never put a limit on their recovery. Not only was it good to inject some much-needed hope into the members of the group, but it was a feel-good moment that Laura and I could share together and help us both make meaning out of what we'd experienced.

So, where's this going? Well, the penny dropped for me after a speech I gave in March 2016, shortly after being laid off from the bank. I was invited to give a keynote at the annual conference of the Utah Speech-Language Hearing Association (USHA), whose members are speech language pathologists and audiologists. Their work is a crucial component of the neuro rehab journey. This event was a game-changer for me.

During the speech, I felt like my connection to the audience was tangible, like I could just about reach out and grab it. Even though there were around three hundred people in the crowd, I felt like I was speaking to each of them one-on-one. They were emotionally engaged, and afterward they gave me a standing ovation and lined up to shake my hand. This felt incredibly good. These are the people who are on the front lines, working every day to help their patients regain critical skills, and they can get burnt out really easily. It's tough work. That day, I felt like I was able to help them feel good about what they do, which I can only hope helped buffer each of them a little bit from the intensity of their jobs.

But for me, the bigger ramification of this event was that, during the speech, I had a sudden epiphany: *I could really make a difference and give back to the brain injury community!* This could be it. This could be the new path that I was looking for. Wow. That was a huge revelation. I loved sharing my story. And I was no stranger to speaking in front of crowds or motivating people—I'd done that for decades as part of my job at the bank. But, at that moment, I saw how my skills, gifts, and circumstances were all pointing toward a new life. Returning to work at the bank had been a triumph for me, for sure—it was a huge marker of my level of recovery and showed me that I could get back to my former self in ways that were rare for TBI survivors. But it wasn't quite the triumph that I thought it was, because what I didn't realize at the time was that I was actually capable of so much more.

Being a successful banker was not enough; it didn't fully draw on my newfound gifts and capabilities. I was proud of the decades of service I'd provided at the bank, but it felt more meaningful to me to help the TBI community who really need the support. At the time, the layoff seemed like a failure, but, in reality, I was getting booted out of complacency so that I could fully launch into a new role. I'd tried so hard to hold on to my life and work as a banker, but I realized I had to get out of my own way. I had to sidestep and see life from a completely new angle. When I did, a new path was revealed.

Once I got it into my noggin that I was going to forge ahead in my new direction as a motivational speaker, I ran with it. I joined the Mountain West Chapter of the National Speakers Association (NSA), which has serious rockstar members, including Dan Clark, whom you might know from his fame as co-author of the mega bestselling Chicken Soup for the Soul series and Chad Hymas, a fellow TBI survivor who came out of the same neuro rehab clinic and whom *Wall Street Journal* called "the most inspirational speaker in the world." I'd met Chad at a talk he'd given to one of the TBI support groups I attend, and he helped me get connected with the NSA and become a professional member.

At one of our chapter meetings, I met a speech ghostwriter and struck up a conversation with her about my memoir. I'd met New York Times Best Selling Author and Hall of Fame Speaker, Dan Clark at The Calliope Writing Coach Writers' Conference where he was doing a keynote, and we hit it off right away. He lit a fire under me. "Get your book written *yesterday*," he said. If you're a speaker, you pretty much *have* to have a book, and so I'd been wanting to rewrite my timeline of recovery booklet "Warmth and a Bad Fish" into a publishable book. The speech writer recommended Sheila Ashdown. After only a few minutes on the phone, Sheila and I connected. It was amazing. After months of looking for a partner to co-write my memoir, I finally found someone who I felt "got me" and understood what I was trying to accomplish in sharing my experience. After years of being self-sufficient and hating to ask for help, I was asking for help all over the place, and it felt good. I'd take all the help I could get, and Sheila was a highly skilled and heartfelt gift sent directly to me.

Starting any new pathway is a challenging endeavor—there's uncertainty, financial instability, and a pretty steep learning curve. But there was also an identity piece. I was still grieving the end of my banking career, and didn't know who I was without it. I didn't feel like I was embodying this new identity; I was calling myself a speaker and a writer almost as if I was convincing myself. It's especially challenging when your new life's purpose hinges on telling strangers your most gory and intimate medical details. If you'd told me before 2016 that I was going to leave behind a lucrative banking career and stand on a stage telling people about the enema that woke me up from a coma, you'd definitely have gotten an "Oh, hell no!" from me. At one of the NSA Chapter meetings, the leader asked newcomers to stand up. And then, he said something to the effect of, "Turn around and run." Of course, that got a good laugh from people, but it's also an acknowledgment of what a challenge it is to be a speaker. It's hard work, with no guarantee of success.

While I may not have wanted to turn around and run, I definitely wasn't all in. I paid my dues, but didn't really fully join, which is uncharacteristic of me. Normally I'd have jumped in with both feet. The first year after joining NSA was a slog, but things eventually started to pick up. I ended up attending Dan Clark's Speakers Bootcamp and joining international bestselling author, Angie Fenimore's, Calliope Writing Coach's program for completing a manuscript. I worked with a family member on developing a website for my new business. I reached out to CEOs and decision-makers I knew, or conversations would happen organically when I ran into colleagues and contacts and told them about my new endeavor. Laura designed business cards for me that had a fish on them—that was always a conversation starter; I got to tell people how I'd crashed my Harley after getting food poisoning from a bad fish. That always shocked people.

So, word got around, I got a few gigs. I was making progress on the new memoir. It started to feel more real. A turning point for me was when I was asked to participate in the NSA's Speaker Showcase, which gives selected speakers a chance to speak in front of talent agents and people looking to hire speakers. It was a big honor that the NSA was putting me forth as a featured member. It was a big-time confidence boost to be among the best of the best that day. Continued personal development with my neuropsychologist Maddie, with a big emphasis on mindfulness, helped me grow to love who I am, without having to rely on a career identity or title for my self-worth. My new direction centered on helping others.

A unique twist in my journey is that starting anew is even more challenging when you have to persuade your reluctant wife to come along for the ride. Of course, Laura was upset about me losing my job, and just as mind-boggled as I was when I couldn't find another one. And with my new aspirations as an inspirational speaker, not only would she have to adjust once again to a major life change-up, but she'd actually have to participate. Relationships are a crucial part of my message. If I was going to speak about how important it was to keep my marriage and family together after TBI, people would definitely want to meet Laura and hear her side of things. She'd not only have to get on board, at some point, she'd have to get on stage.

25

In 2016, Laura and I went back to Coeur d'Alene to mark the five-year anniversary of my accident. This time around, we drove in a car, with seatbelts on. Oh, and I was conscious. I'd been bugging Laura for a long time to revisit the crash site and meet the people who'd saved my life at Kootenai to thank them. Previously, she'd give me a look and change the subject. And then one day, she gave me the okay. Her post-traumatic stress had healed to a point where she could stomach the idea of revisiting the scene.

I contacted Kootenai's marketing department and told them my idea: I was coming up for the five-year anniversary, and I wanted to meet the CEO of the hospital, the surgeons, and the rest of the critical care team. Kootenai took it from there. Not only did they arrange the meeting, they turned it into a full-on event, complete with media coverage. It was wild.

When we arrived August 15, 2016, exactly five years from the day that life flight landed on the roof of Kootenai Health, John Ness, the CEO of the hospital, said jokingly, "Well, now that you've got us all gathered together, what can we do for you?"

I said, "John, we're here, Laura and I, just to tell you face-to-face what an amazing hospital you have, how scared Laura was to be here, and to express how grateful we are for what your team did for us—for me and my family. I read all of the charting notes from my stay at Kootenai Health, and I know your medical professionals worked endlessly to save my life and give me a fighting chance to recover from my gruesome accident. Thank you."

And he replied, "I can count on one hand how many times patients have come back to me and said 'thank you.'" Apparently, people just don't do that. Former patients rarely show up in person, drive from another state, just to say thank you.

As soon as the critical care team came in and we saw them, and I saw Chauntae, Kelsy, Dr. Ganz, Dr. Bowen and the rest of the team. It was just hugs and tears. We couldn't stop hugging each other. It was like meeting old friends for the first time. They kept saying "Greg, it's so good to see you upright." To me, that seemed like a weird phrasing, but it makes perfect sense from their perspective. I was still in and out of my coma and non-weight-bearing when I left Kootenai, so they just saw a little slice of me while I was at my worst. They didn't get to experience my real personality during the time I was in their care. I was just weird and out of it. The last time they saw me, they couldn't have even guessed how I was going to recover, I was so out of my mind. They wouldn't have taken a bet that I'd reach the level of recovery that I have, or get my job back, and that Laura and I would still be together and in love after all we'd been through. They were just blown away.

It was especially meaningful to me that I got to "meet" Chauntae, who was my primary neurology nurse during my stay in the intensive care unit. She performed my initial evaluation and kept track of my severe coma rating and my reactions, which were minimal that first day. She would say my name loudly and push hard on my sternum to try to get me to open my eyes for a few seconds, flashing her medical light across my eyes to check my reactions. Chauntae was very comforting to both Laura and me, and she held my hand while I was unconscious. In her notes, she wrote that, after several hours, I started to sense when she was next to me on her rounds. Sometimes I reached out for her hand if she didn't immediately take mine. She became my connection to the medical world I was immersed in.

In the middle of my first night, Dr. Ganz asked for another CT scan, and Chauntae took me to the imaging room. She wrote in her notes that she helped transfer me to the CT bed, which caused a tremendous amount of pain to my open wounds and head injury. She said I tried to cry out "Come on!" but I had an intubation tube down my throat. I became extremely agitated and thrashed on the table. They tried running the CT scan, but the films were blurry. Then, Chauntae reached over and held my hand and softly talked to me before the technician took a new set of scans. Her presence and kind words calmed me, and I held still enough for them to get clear pictures.

When I later had gathered up all of my hospital notes to write "Warmth and a Bad Fish," I read Chauntae's notes, and I had tears in my eyes. A complete stranger had carried me through physical agony during those first critical twenty-four hours of my recovery. Chauntae was endeared to me even though I don't remember her. When I finally got to meet her in person, we hugged each other tightly, tears streaming from our eyes. I didn't want to let go.

The entire ICU neurology team cared deeply for Laura and me. They watched over both of us during the hardest time in our lives. They constantly asked Laura if she was okay and brought her treats and coffee. Their actions speak more than I can articulate. I don't physically remember the events of my time at Kootenai, but their presence and internal connections still live with me. I hold them close to my being. I later learned from Laura that the team of neurology nurses in the ICU were a very tight group. I can see why they were close friends after being the recipient of their heartfelt nurturing over countless hours.

I told the Kootenai's critical care team and executives that I'd felt a great burden of debt ever since my accident, but someone—and I wish I could remember who—told me that my burden was misplaced. This was the first time that anybody had ever corrected me on that point. They said, "We've been paid. You're trying to repay us for something that we've already been paid for." They encouraged me to let it go. "You don't need this on your shoulders."

Kelsy, who was our checkout nurse at Kootenai, was there too, and after embracing us, she shared with us a blog post she'd written about working with me and Laura the last two nights we were at Kootenai Health:

> The patient had short-term memory loss and woke up one night at 3:30am asking where [he was], what happened, and can [he] talk to [his] spouse, please? I finally got a hold of [his] spouse (I felt awful for calling at that terrible time, but it was clear the patient needed so badly to hear that familiar voice). When I put the patient on the phone with [his] spouse, I heard [his] voice crack, tears welling in [his] eyes, that moment of knowing it was all going to be okay just by hearing that well-known voice of a partner.
>
> When I took them, patient and spouse, out to the car to meet up with their transportation home early in the morning the next day, my breath caught in my chest. Their love for one another, and staying by each other's side, in sickness and health, was so profound. I helped the patient into the car, touching [his] arm, telling [him], "It was a pleasure caring for you." I turned and hugged [his] spouse. It was a special moment of knowing that a hug was needed. The patient's spouse said, "Thank you so much. Have a great day. Actually, have a great life." I said, "You too." We knew we'd probably never see each other again, so it was fitting.
>
> They left an imprint on my heart. It was a much-needed feeling of making a difference. As I drove home I almost missed my exit through my teary eyes. And this is why I'm a nurse.[1]

Kelsy's care for us and her words are embedded within me.

At first, I didn't know what to do with the thought of letting go of my debt burden. But I thought about it and thought about it, and... I felt relieved. They *had* already been paid; each of them had chosen that career in order to help people like

---

[1] Kelsy's blog post originally referred to me as "they" to protect my anonymity, but I edited here for readability.

me. It's what they do for a living. They're trained for it. They're ready to save lives. They're ready to treat patients like me. They told me they receive their satisfaction in watching me and others recover—and they get satisfaction in getting their paychecks. I realized I could relate, what with my volunteer work. I didn't get paid in money, obviously, but I got rewarded with unforgettable feel-good moments. If the survivors or caregivers I mentored felt like they owed me anything, I'd say it was nonsense. So, when I heard it from the team at Kootenai, I was genuinely persuaded. I had a mindset shift. It was an epiphany. I wouldn't say that all the weight was lifted off of me, but I didn't feel like I had to repay it all, even though I didn't understand why I'd received the gifts that I had. As Kelsy said, "They left an imprint on my heart." Maybe that's enough—or at least a portion paid.

* * *

While in Coeur d'Alene, Laura and I also visited the crash site. I had Google-mapped the route we'd taken, referencing pictures of the crash site, trying to figure out the exact place where I left the road. Some of the photos showed my tire tracks in the gravel shoulder where I'd started to veer off. I inspected those photos for landmarks like reflector posts, guard rails, trees, and bushes that would help me pinpoint the exact place. I took screenshots of Google Maps and all the crash pics and brought them with us to Coeur d'Alene.

The day we drove out, it was mid-morning on a mild day in August. The weather was nice, with billowy clouds floating across the sky. We'd only driven about forty minutes from Coeur d'Alene when all the sudden we were there. That surprised me. In my mind, I'd been thinking the crash site was out in the middle of nowhere. But really it was just a short drive from Coeur d'Alene. It was a rural road with not much traffic, just two lanes most of the time, though this portion happened to have a passing lane. We'd almost made it to Coeur d'Alene on the day of the crash.

We got to the place I'd marked on Google Maps, made a U-turn, and pulled over to park on the side of the road. I could see the exact spot where Laura had parked her bike that dreadful day. I literally had the pictures with me—seven or eight pictures that I'd pieced together to mark the place. Some pictures were from bystanders and some were Google Maps screenshots. And we found it.

When we got out of the car, I thought, "Wow, this is where most of the emotions are going to come up." But that's not how it was. Instead, Laura and I immediately turned into detectives. We'd found the spot where my bike had left the road, and so then we wanted to find where my bike had ended up. Using the pictures, we hunted around and found it.

"That's it," Laura said, pointing. "That's where you were. Underneath your Harley. Right there. I sat on that rock, cradling you."

We both started fiddling around in the nearby rocks, and right away we started unearthing all kinds of stuff. Looking closely, we could see that the whole area around where I'd crashed was scattered with debris from my bike and bits and pieces of emergency medical supplies. One of the first things we found was the cord from my iPod that had been connected from my vest to my Harley stereo when I crashed. Then we found the cigarette lighter from the Ultra; I'd hit the ground so hard, the cigarette lighter had been ejected. That would have to have taken immense force because they're rubber sealed to keep them dry.

Laura found my bloody socks, which had been cut off by the first responders and tossed aside. It was shocking to find this stuff; some of it was actually on my person in an intimate way—my socks! The socks I'd been wearing the moment my entire life changed, just there, strewn about at the crash site.

It seemed like every rock we pulled up, we'd find something. I found the owner's manual to my bike, its pages ragged and stiff from being exposed to the elements. I found rags and the shattered spray bottle of cleaner for my helmet visor from the glove box attached to my right engine guard. I found the chrome polisher that I used to wipe down my bike at the end of the day. I found the lens cover from my right turn signal—that's one of the ways you customize Harleys, is with custom lens covers. The craziest thing I found were two white fairing pieces, v-shaped with a point, about eight to ten inches long apiece. The fairing was the sleek plastic shell that covered the front the bike, and these two pieces had broken off in the mayhem and were embedded straight down into the dirt, where they'd stayed for five years. They'd been forced down through the rocks and into the ground. These two pieces of the fairing seemed especially meaningful because they told me the story of how the crash must have gone down. Remember, they were laid to rest, side by side, during horrific moments of the crash and we unearthed them for closure.

We spent a couple hours at the site, walking the fifty-yard path from where my bike left the road to where it reached its demise, reconstructing the crash trajectory and collecting physical evidence. Laura retold me the story of seeing the colored globes of gumballs covering the grassy hillside along the path my bike must have taken. We walked from the point where my bike's tracks left the road, made the first impact with the rock ditch, through the hillside, and back down to the final crash into the rocks where we found all the debris. I'd heard all different variations and speculations about how the crash had gone down, but the physical evidence told me a story that helped crystalize it in my mind.

It was fascinating. It was both an archaeological treasure hunt and a detective investigation for us. We picked up all the bits and pieces we could find, everything crumpled and weathered and caked in dirt, and put it all in the trunk of the car to take back with us. It was surreal to collect these shards of items that had once been well-known. It reminded me of how, when we were in Coeur d'Alene the first time around, Laura was given a cardboard box full of the gear that I'd been wearing during the accident. It had all been cut off me. An extremely expensive black leather jacket, cut to pieces. My life as a Harley rider began the day I walked into the dealership and saw all that shiny gear and ended with all that gear being scraped up, torn, covered in blood, mud, and vomit, and ultimately cut from my body by EMTs and paramedics. One piece of equipment that wasn't in the trunk was my helmet. Jimmy had salvaged it. I will always have reverence for my Harley half-helmet with the blazing skulls. It saved my life. I wouldn't be writing this memoir if it hadn't been strapped to my huge noggin correctly, protecting me from the dime-sized point of a lava rock on August 15th of 2011, after I ate a bad fish.

I didn't know if going to the crash site would be a good idea for either Laura or myself. I was worried that it would be emotional for us both. I assumed that I'd lose it and break into tears at the crash site, and I was even more concerned that Laura's post-traumatic stress could be triggered. Surprisingly, that wasn't the case at all. "It didn't even faze me," Laura said. "It was like a treasure hunt." We both were totally focused on discovery and re-creating the play-by-play of the crash. I'd heard about the event so many times, but it was different being there myself (well, there and conscious). To walk there, to walk through the grassy hill, walk across the bed of lava rock, to sit on the rock that Laura had sat on while she was saving my life. I'd re-created with it with pictures and Google Maps, but it was completely different to be there physically. I had always wondered about that place.

Coeur d'Alene is more beautiful than was described to me. The lakes, rivers, and forests are majestic and cover all your eyes can see. Nothing is left bare. Laura and I are from the desert and used to amazing mountain ranges, surrounded by dry valleys. Coeur d'Alene is green and lush, and its lakes and rivers are wide and crystal clear. As we took a day driving around Lake Coeur d'Alene—like we had planned to five years earlier on our Harleys—the immensity of lost opportunity hit me.

Our adventure in 2011 would have eclipsed Laura's expectations and mine. My crash ruined it. But having a chance to drive back five years later was something I desperately needed, emotionally and psychologically. From the very beginning of the ordeal, it unnerved me that I had no memory of it and being there closed the chapter for me.

26

After we reconnected with the team at Kootenai Health, they did Laura and I the honor of asking us to serve as spokespeople at their Festival of Trees black-tie fundraising gala in November 2016. As part of this, we would deliver a keynote address. The Festival of Trees is part of a big Thanksgiving-time celebration put on by The Coeur d'Alene Resort.

As part of the festivities, Kootenai Health was putting on a gala that would raise funds to be used to rebuild the hospital's emergency room and operating room facilities. Of course, being the competitive people we are, Laura and I wanted to help Kootenai break their fundraising record. In my mind, I thought that meant helping them reach $75,000 or $100,000. But there's a lot of money and celebrity in Coeur d'Alene. And so, the week of the gala, we found out that the fundraising record to beat was four times what we were used to on a gross revenue level (more than twice as much on a net basis). Laura and I had helped with fund-raising gala events in Salt Lake, so we weren't strangers to this sort of thing. But the scale was a whole new world. The silent auction was filled with multi-thousand-dollar items that wowed us as we walked around. But as soon as I heard Kootenai's past record, I was all in. I wanted to beat it. That's my natural orientation.

I don't feel like there's anything I can't do, but this felt like a particularly high-pressure situation. I already hold myself to high standards, but in this case I felt a great pressure to deliver big results for Kootenai. These were the people who saved my life and gave me a chance to regain all that I did. Everything they did gave me the opportunities that I have now. If they hadn't saved me, I wouldn't be with my family, walking and on a new pathway. They could have asked me to do anything, and I would have said, "Hell yeah, we're in. Whatever the record, we'll beat it." That's my personality. Of course, no one at Kootenai put an iota of pressure on me— it was all me. And you know Laura. She is as competitive as I am. Or more.

Post-TBI, I have memory deficits that I contend with every day. Memorization is hugely taxing on my brain. But I was determined to memorize my speech so I could be up on that stage, microphone in hand, no papers. I wanted to create an immersive, enthralling experience—not interrupt myself and break the flow by having to look down at my notes. I had to get up on that stage and deliver the kind of inspirational speech that would have these folks, the upper crust of Coeur d'Alene, opening up their wallets and purses and pulling out their credit cards and donating at a much grander scale than what I'd witnessed in Salt Lake.

Laura and I had done a lot of work ahead of time in the weeks leading up to the gala, but the speech wasn't finalized. We wrote, rewrote, and practiced on the flight. Practiced non-stop in the hotel room. An hour before we were about to go on stage, we were still figuring out some basics like which of us would lead us off. We weren't eating nutritiously—we just grabbed whatever crap was on hand. We were staying up late. I imposed on myself an unbelievable amount of pressure to please everyone at Kootenai, but especially Dr. Ganz, Dr. Bowen, and the critical care team. I knew they wouldn't put me under that pressure, but I didn't care. I just wanted to hear them say, "Greg, you're doing a good job," just like I wanted to hear when I woke up from a coma and was thriving on positive feedback. It would have killed me to not achieve our fundraising goals.

Laura and I just about brought down the house, if I do say so myself. She shared her experience watching me crash, saving me, and keeping me alive onsite and bagging me in the life flight. She tugged on the attendees' heartstrings, hard, when she explained her pain in the ER. She praised the incredible medical care we received by the surgeons and the critical care team that saved my life and put my body back together. When it was time to close, Laura passed me the mic. I stood in front of that crowd and said, "You will never regret what you're about to do. Reach into your wallets and purses and donate tonight. The money will save your life someday. Or the life of someone in your family. Or will save the life of one of your neighbors, or someone who works with you, or someone you know in your community. Or will save the life of someone like me, a stranger who just happens to be riding through Coeur d'Alene. You will never regret it." People were bawling and clapping, and Laura and I were just about ready to fall over because we could hardly see through our tears as we walked off the stage.

It was an inspirational and moving moment that will be permanently embedded within Laura and me. We worked hard to create a dynamic motivational speech that allowed us to speak from our hearts and souls and challenge people to reach into their wallets and donate unbelievable amounts. Before the night was even out, the rough numbers were tabulated and we knew we'd helped the foundation break their record. Wow.

About a week after the gala, back in Salt Lake City, the Brain Injury Alliance of Utah threw a Christmas party for brain injury survivors and caregivers. It also happened to be Laura's birthday. I was still feeling exhausted from traveling to Coeur d'Alene and speaking the week before. I was wiped out, physically and mentally. But I knew I couldn't skip the party. Even though my brain was beyond fatigued, I wanted to put my best self forward and make sure that Laura's birthday was a special day for her. We got to the party venue early to help set up and then we ended up staying late, so it was a long day. The party was a great time—I even got the emcee to announce Laura's birthday, and we all sang "Happy Birthday" to her. But it was also crowded and noisy and overwhelming, with lots of conversations going on, lots of lights, and a group singing Christmas carols. By the time we were ready to head home, I was spent—I was beyond spent—but I did my best to maintain my composure.

When we finally got to the car, Laura got in the driver's seat to drive home, as she usually does when I'm tired. But then she got a FaceTime call from one of our kids who was calling to wish her a happy birthday. I didn't want her to have to miss the call. "Let me drive," I said. We were only about ten miles from home, and it was only 9:30.

Huge mistake.

Coming into downtown, I took the freeway offramp, and I had a "TBI moment." I blanked out. I don't have any memory from the time I got on the ramp until the moment I heard Laura scream, "GREG!" I was driving *fast*, at freeway speed, toward the center cement divide and another car that was exiting. I slammed on the brakes, which initiated the antilock braking system, and turned the steering wheel to the right as hard as I could. I missed killing us by inches.

When we got home and pulled into the garage, I rolled out of the car and into a human ball on the cement floor, and sobbed. Laura wanted to take me to the hospital, but I was adamant that she not do that. I was afraid my license would be taken away—I was sure that's what would happen. I thought I'd lose everything I'd gained in my recovery and have to start from scratch again—speech therapy, occupational therapy, neuropsychology—to recover from what had just happened. I was afraid I'd have to take the driving exam again. I was beyond myself, lying on the floor of the garage. But we'd just had this traumatic experience and Laura said, "I have to call Dr. Dodds." She helped me get up and inside the house and covered me with a blanket. I was in shock, for obvious reasons. She called Dr. Dodds, but he was out of town, so she scheduled a time for me to talk with him on Monday.

When we got on the phone a couple days later, Dr. Dodds said something to the effect of, "Greg, this was a TBI moment. You know better than to drive when you're fatigued, right?" He said it's extremely common for a TBI survivor to have a "phase out" or "blackout." I didn't lose consciousness; I just lost track of what was happening. It's common with the combination of fatigue and sensory overstimulation I'd experienced that night. Especially since I hadn't taken care of myself the week prior and I hadn't really prepared for the evening.

I knew I'd made a huge mistake in offering to drive when I was as wiped out as I was that night. I'd almost killed my best friend and lover—and myself—in order to learn that lesson, and it's a mistake I won't make again. I promised Dr. Dodds I'd never do it again, and I have not—nor will I ever. For a TBI survivor, taking the wheel while extremely fatigued is like taking the wheel while intoxicated; it's an awful thing to do. The worst thing you can be doing is driving while a TBI "phase out" happens. Dr. Dodds told me not to drive on the freeway for a while. He had me come into his office for tests, and then he directed me to see my neuropsychologist, Maddie, weekly to work through and understand what had happened.

I started the neuro psych therapy sessions with Maddie right away, and we spent months talking through what had happened. It was hard to come to grips with the fact that I'd almost killed us. It's hard to write about it now. But I had to figure out how to come to terms with it and get beyond it. To this day, though I'm able to acknowledge the situation, I'm not sure I've forgiven myself yet. But I've looked the situation in the face. It happened. I've shared my feelings of failure and admitted what I did wrong.

I can't go back in time and change what happened, but I can go forward in a new and different way. I did this by making two commitments. The first was that I'd never drive in a severely fatigued state ever again. That was the easy one.

The second commitment was harder and more complicated: I committed to accepting myself as a TBI survivor—and the reality of what that entails. I had to get myself into a place where I could fully understand and accept myself and my new place in the world. I was a TBI survivor, and even though I'd made huge strides in my recovery, I had weaknesses and limitations. I had to plan my life around that fact. With Maddie's help, I learned to cope. We did mindfulness training in session and I did it on my own. We used cognitive behavioral therapy (CBT) to understand my limitations and get in tune with my body and its boundaries. I talked a lot with Laura. I walked a lot. I pulled back from volunteering and participating in groups and focused on my own recovery for a while.

* * *

I'd gotten myself into this dire situation because I'd pushed myself too hard in preparation for a speech. I could never do that again. Part of the problem is that I'd forced myself to memorize my speech for the Kootenai gala, and I'd taxed my brain in doing so. I put myself under so much pressure, I broke myself. I sure as hell couldn't do that again.

But I had to wonder, if I was dependent on using notes, could I be the kind of speaker I wanted to be? I admire speakers who don't use notes and who seem to seamlessly move from one story to the next. Without notes, a speaker can be fully engaged in the moment and fully present with the audience. When they pause, it's purposeful—it's a dramatic pause or an intentional moment designed to let an idea land. They're not pausing because they've forgotten what to say and need to look at their notes. To me, that seemed amateur. And if I needed to use notes, I perceived that to mean I was limited in how effective or successful of a speaker I could be. If I couldn't be as polished as other speakers, maybe that would limit the caliber of gigs I could get, especially in professional environments. I've got a message, and I love to connect with people, but if I break that contact because I have to look down at my notes during a powerful part of my speech, does that dilute the power of the message? It's distracting, for sure. It makes me question my career, and whether there's any hope of true, lasting, big success. I have a dream I want to pursue, and I fear I might not be up for the task.

Seeing the intense pressure and stress I put myself under, and fearing for my well-being, Laura has asked me many times: "Are you sure speaking is the right route for you?" In my lowest moments, I'm ready to throw in the towel and call it quits. But on days when I have a more optimistic perspective, I think a more constructive question is, "I've got a message and I love to connect with people. How do I get creative and figure out how to do that without harming myself?" Because, when I think about it, I've seen plenty of great speakers who killed it on stage *and* used notes. No big deal! I'd made it into a big deal because I wasn't accepting myself, and I was comparing myself with others. The underlying purpose—my why—is to help brain injury survivors and caregivers overcome the same obstacles I faced, provide hope, and deliver gratitude, for relationships to be nourished. I have to do this to be whole.

Lori and LeeAnne, my EVP friends at my former bank, asked me to speak at their annual Retail Affiliate Bancorp Conference. It was a tremendous honor, and felt good to be home again amongst my banking peers. They asked me to share my experience of overcoming horrendous obstacles after waking from my coma. My story melded with their banking objectives that year. Afterward, bankers lined up to talk with me. They shared that they missed me. I joked, "Not as much as I miss you guys." Man, that was a feel-good day. I've since been asked to speak at the bank several times. Each brings me back to my "Banker Bob" roots.

One of the many lessons I've learned throughout this TBI rollercoaster is that if you're not in a place of acceptance, you're in purgatory. I've seen this in a lot of the survivors and caregivers I've interacted with over the years. Some people haven't accepted themselves and their path post-brain injury. They're holding on to the past and comparing themselves unfavorably to what they used to be or have or do. Their experience of the present is one of inescapable remorse and a focus on their limitations.

When I meet these folks in recovery groups, I ask them, "What if you could say that the old pathway was what it was, and the new pathway could be full of wonderment and new opportunities you just haven't seen yet?" What I know to be true for myself, and the hope I carry for other TBI survivors and their caregivers, is that when we get out of our own way and allow life to turn the corner, new opportunities can materialize. I never knew I'd be up in front of groups of people, speaking about recovery, helping people when they need help the most. If I gave up on my speaking calling because my TBI has forced me to do things a bit differently than I would have preferred, I would have lost out on some of the most incredibly joyful, meaningful, connected experiences of my life.

I went through a particularly down period near the end of 2017. Speaking opportunities were cropping up and then disappearing, I had gargantuan kidney stones (with hospital bills to match), and financial worries hung over my head. In a single day, I could spend a morning having a feel-good experience with someone in my TBI community, and then spend the afternoon wading through the details of huge financial decisions like whether or not to sell our house—all while battling fatigue—with the fact that my analytical brain doesn't work so well. I was exhausted by the constant emotional whiplash.

I acknowledge that my analytical cognitive capacities have weakened, I get fatigued easily, and migraines are reaching an all-time high. And if that isn't enough, freakin' depression gets the better of me at times. I spiral. Sometimes I want to say, "Haven't you slapped me around enough already?"

I was in the midst of all these ups-and-downs when I was invited to be a guest on a podcast hosted by psychologist Dr. Paul Jenkins, who I met through the National Speakers Association. He sponsored me through my nomination to the board of directors of the Mountain West Chapter of the association. I was waffling. I didn't know if I had the confidence to join the board. I didn't know if I had the cognitive bandwidth or energy to handle the responsibilities. I was dark. I was low. I was inches from giving up on the whole endeavor.

When I confessed to Paul that I was having second thoughts about being part of the board, he encouraged me. During a break in recording the podcast, he told me that his wife is a speech pathologist, and he reminded me of the story I told during my nomination speech, of the epiphany I'd had while delivering a speech to the Utah

Speech-Language Hearing Association. Connecting with those people—who'd dedicated their lives to the very profession that had made it possible for me to even be up on a stage giving a speech—had made me realize I could make a difference through speaking. Paul asked me to share the feelings I experienced while giving that speech. I started crying in the middle of doing the damn radio show. Paul's question plugged me right back into my purpose and motivation. Just because my purpose was obscured by the ten tons of shit I was dealing with didn't mean that it was gone. I'd just lost sight of it for a bit. I said, "Dr. Paul, please give your wife a hug from me to her and say 'thank you' for all she does in the brain injury community."

* * *

Success in life doesn't happen when we focus on our limitations. It happens when we identify our strengths and play to them. This is what everyone should be doing, of course, but it's all the more obvious when you're a TBI survivor. I know some TBI survivors probably look at me and compare themselves to me, and I get it—I've done it with other speakers and authors.

It seems like everywhere I look, I'm seeing people who are worlds ahead of me. As TBI survivors, we're prone to depression, and making comparisons is an easy way to spiral down into a deep, dark rabbit hole. It's life as viewed through a lens of loss. It's also not helpful to try to make ourselves become who we used to be, which isn't possible anyway. It's a fool's errand and a surefire way to misery. Instead, as we accept the new person we've become, with all the tragedy and beauty and limitations and possibilities that are wrapped up in that, the result is joy and healing. We create goals that are centered around who we are now; we track those goals and see how far we've come. We compare ourselves to our *current* self—not to a past self or other people. This is our survivor's key to progress.

Of course, if someone isn't motivated to make new goals, there's nothing I or anybody can do to inject them with self-motivation. Caregivers, family, friends, and medical professionals can't force them. When it comes to self-motivation, you've either got it or you don't; but I do feel that there are ways to wake up the self-drive that is within each of us. We all have a fire within us, and there are ways to stoke that fire. I've had moments of connection with people who are at their darkest times and lowest points, and have given up. I can feel the depths of despair within them. After connecting with them and chatting, and just having a moment of time with them, I can feel their spark awaken. I can sense the glimmer of hope that arises. It's magical.

In 2017, I had the honor of presenting at a large brain injury conference. Laura and I did a breakout session titled "Nurturing Relationships after Brain Injury" and then I gave the afternoon keynote address. After the keynote, a woman came up to me. I was still up on the stage, and she came up the edge of it, bawling. I kneeled down and hugged her.

She said, "Greg, I was at the breakout session—and I hated you afterward."

This was a real shocker, because that's not typically the kind of feedback I get! "Oh my gosh!" I exclaimed.

But then she said, "But don't worry. I listened to this speech you gave and I adore you now."

I asked, "What'd I say that made you hate me?"

"You had *everything* after your Harley crash," she said. "You had the support of family and loved ones and this network around you. I had nothing. My family disengaged from me. My children are addicts, and they don't want anything to do with me. I've lost everything. I've given up hope for everything. I looked at you up there with your wife and I just hated you."

I was sad and distraught to hear her say this to me. We were both crying and hugging.

She continued, "After you spoke this afternoon and shared what you've been through and all of your trials, and all that you've lost—losing your career and having to start over with neuropsychology—I could feel you reaching out to me as if you were talking directly to me. And I love that you were being open and honest with me. And when you said that we should reach out again to our loved ones and nurture our relationships and try to give our loved ones a chance again, and build on those relationships that are the most meaningful, I made a decision. I'm going to reach out to my children and show them my love that I have inside of me that's so deep and hidden. I love you for that, Greg." My heart just broke. "I went from hating you to loving you." I lost it—right there—on stage.

I've also found that motivation is a two-way street. It's not just about me standing up on a platform and telling my story, inspiring people. I experience major ups and down like any other person, and any other TBI survivor, and it's the audience members who lift *me* up, not the other way around.

Months after speaking at the brain injury conference, I was contacted by another person who'd attended the event. She wanted to meet me for coffee. When she told me her name over the phone, it wasn't familiar to me, but as soon as I saw her at the coffee shop, I remembered the very moment that she and I had made eye contact during my speech. I'm going to call her "Gail." Gail had a bright, unforgettable smile. We'd hugged that day of the event, but hadn't spoken in any depth. But later, she felt compelled to reach out.

As we sat with our coffees, she told me her life story, which was heart wrenching. She'd been sexually and physically abused for a long time by close family members and had suffered concussions and TBIs from being knocked around and hit. She'd never healed from that experience. Though she'd gone on to create a brilliant career in a creative profession, Gail always felt lost and had attempted suicide multiple times. She spent her life avoiding romantic or close relationships with men, because she felt she couldn't trust any of them. As you can imagine, I was heartbroken to hear her story.

There was a moment in that speech when I said, "We need to get out of this basement, to get out of this introversion, and to reach beyond ourselves and share our love with others, to share experiences, to reach out and find friendships and communities and repair relationships. To share our warmth with others." I remember locking eyes with Gail and creating a connection just as I said those words. And it hit home with Gail too. When we met over coffee, she told me, at that moment, she knew it was time to start trying to trust men again. Trusting in general.

Wow.

I reached over and hugged Gail, and I said, "You don't even know how much that means to me, to hear you say that my speech was good for you. But more importantly, our connection was heartfelt."

Gail said that when she heard me speak, she realized it was her time to give back and to find a community of women who'd been through what she'd been through, and to find a purpose, to give others hope. Of course, I was totally losing it while she was talking—partly because her experience was so moving, and partly because of the healing that I was experiencing just then myself.

Gail asked, "Will you always remember that connection that you had with me on that stage?"

"How could I ever forget?"

I absolutely cannot wait to see what Gail does with her life, and how many women she impacts with her work, and how many of these types of conversations she'll have in coffee shops in the future. She had already motivated one person—me. We later ran into each other again at another brain injury event, and the breadth of our connection was as strong as that moment in the crowded event center. Yes, Gail, I'll always remember. I will never forget you.

I feel a sense of wonderment when these things happen; it's the ultimate form of interconnection from one human to another. These are stand-out moments. I wish I could put them into a snow globe and encapsulate them forever. After having these moments and helping these TBI survivors, the satisfaction I felt from booking million-dollar deals became secondary—and the challenges and growing pains of my new pathway feel ultimately worthwhile.

27

The greatest lesson I ever learned in speech therapy had nothing to do with relearning how to speak. One day, not long after I'd been released from IMC, I came waltzing into my speech therapy session and sat down in a huff.

Kim, my speech therapist, asked, "What's wrong?"

"I just had an argument with Laura," I said. I had no idea what we'd even argued about, since I had no short-term memory, but it was probably something stupid.

Whatever it was, Kim let me complain about it for about two minutes before she interrupted me and said, "Get up. Get your walker. Where's Laura?" I told her Laura was out in the car.

Kim said, "Ask Laura to get out of the car and stand next to you. Don't *tell* her— *ask* her. Then, number one, say 'I love you.' Number two, say 'I'm sorry.' Then, number three, thank her for all that she is doing to take care of you. Number four, give her a hug."

Well, that changed my attitude.

Kim was really stern with me that day. She had me reiterate her instructions several times until I could remember them all. Finally, I got it, and I got my walker and went out to find Laura in the parking lot, waiting for me in the car. Gently, I asked her to get out, and I did exactly what Kim told me to do.

Laura was confused. "What are you doing?" she asked.

"I can't believe I did that, honey. I'm so sorry. I love you. Thank you, sweetie, for everything you're doing for me." We hugged each other for a long time, and then I hobbled back inside for the rest of my session with Kim.

And, for the record, during the course of writing this book, Laura reminded me what we'd fought about that day... Soon after being released from IMC, a friend of ours named Cathy, who is an artist, was showing her work in a gallery. Cathy's husband had been a huge help to us in the immediate aftermath of the crash—he'd flown to Spokane, to the Harley dealership, and ridden Laura's bike back to Salt Lake City. And so, when it turned out Cathy was showing her art, Laura wanted to stop by the opening to support her. It was a gorgeous fall day, sixty degrees or so. She offered to take me along for the ride, and I agreed to go, but after she'd loaded me and my walker into the back of her car and drove to the gallery, I decided I didn't want to go in. I wanted to go home, *now*. Laura said, "Okay, Greg, we'll go home. Let me just run in for a minute and say hi to Cathy really quickly." But I wasn't having it. In the span of time it took for Laura to run in and say hello, I became *pissed*. Nothing could console me. I was hell-bent.

When we got home, I grabbed my car keys even though I couldn't drive and couldn't even walk yet. In the past, when Laura and I had a hot moment, I'd grab my motorcycle or the car or go for a walk to get away and cool down. So, I walked out the kitchen door, onto the deck, threw my walker down the short staircase, scooted down on my butt, and picked the walker back up. I hopped across the stone path leading to the garage and then got into my car and turned it on, using my uninjured left foot on the brake. I turned on the big band music my dad used to love, because I couldn't handle my preferred music yet—Rush, Metallica. And I just sat there. I'd lost control over everything in my life, and this was one way of grabbing something back.

What I didn't know was that Laura had watched all of this without me knowing. She stood there, looking at me and thinking, "Where the heck does he think he's going?" But she didn't interfere. She let me have my "control" moment as my caregiver, lover, best friend. Without having any training or mentoring herself, she knew what to do. This was one of Laura's greatest and most amazing caregiver moments. Over a nothing argument that I don't even remember.

After five or ten minutes, when I was done, Laura helped me get back into the house. She was tender and loving and didn't care about a stupid, meaningless argument. But I apparently cared. I was pissed all day long and woke up still feeling frustrated the next day. That's what I was complaining about when I walked into my speech therapy session and Kim set me straight.

It was an awakening moment for me. It was the first time I realized that I was a TBI survivor and I had a TBI caregiver. Those terms were foreign to me. But Kim had turned on the light for me, and I would never forget the lesson. Laura was working her butt off for me as my caregiver, waiting on me hand and foot and lovingly taking care of every little thing that I needed. I would have been lost without her. I knew then that I had to be mindful to always show her my appreciation and nurture our relationship. That lesson had nothing to do with relearning how to talk, but it was my greatest lesson in all of my recovery.

When it comes to TBI survivorship, it's possible that the injury to the brain is secondary to the injury to our relationships. Everywhere you look, the stats are dire—remember, a common one you hear is that seventy-five percent of marriages end in divorce when one spouse suffers a TBI. And it's not just marriages. Whether it's because a TBI survivor has had a personality change, is unable to go back to work, is immobilized, or becomes reclusive, it's exceedingly common for our relationships to wither and die.

For me, I spent the first years after my recovery intensely focused on a few key areas: keeping my marriage and family together, relearning critical skills like reading, writing, speaking, and walking, and getting my job back. I was so single-mindedly focused on those areas, when I eventually looked up a few years later, I saw that my communities had dried up. Everything I focused on, I achieved. But everything else was collateral damage. People need attention. Even though no one could fault me for needing to focus on myself in the aftermath of a brain injury, it still meant I had nothing to give to other relationships, and I didn't even try. I went inward. I gave up on people, and they gave up on me.

For Laura, her world shrank too, but for different reasons. She kept wondering, "Where is everybody? Where are all those dinners that people are supposed to drop off when something goes wrong?" It wasn't until later that she realized that she'd pushed people away. She'd wanted privacy to deal with what we had in front of us, but she got way too much of a good thing. On top of that she was dealing with shock and PTSD. She's the first to admit now that, if she had to do it all over again, she'd throw open the doors and accept all the help that people had wanted to give. She says, "*Yes* and *thank you* would have been my two favorite phrases." We honor the people in our lives by allowing them to help us. People don't face these kinds of tragedies every day, thankfully, and so most of us aren't prepared to meet them when they do arrive on our doorsteps. People are lost. They want to help, but don't want to intrude. Laura's message to caregivers is, "Say yes. Accept the help. When we help someone, we receive the gift of love in return. Allow those around you to receive that gift."

Though it was exceedingly painful to look up and realize how alone we felt—and just how much we'd been in charge of creating that aloneness—we allowed that pain to be a wakeup call. We needed to find new community, new purpose, new connection.

Fortunately for Laura and me, community was waiting for us. Laura found some sorely needed community with other caregivers. Not only did it make her feel empowered to start the group herself, but it was healing for her to be around people who understood. She said that words caregivers use to describe themselves are *neglected*, *isolated*, *abandoned*, *disrespected*, *ignored*, *unsupported*, *lonely*, and *misunderstood*. Yikes.

143

Like Laura, none of those people signed up to become a brain injury caregiver; it was a role thrust upon them by circumstance. Caregivers are at high risk of burnout because they have zero training for the gig and are given very little support. Her caregiver group was and is a haven where she and others like her can share their experiences without judgment. They can come into the group and say, straight up, "This was a really screwed-up day." All the caregivers have been there. They don't need to sugarcoat things, because they realize their frustrations don't mean they don't care. When Laura first started meeting with other caregivers, the veterans—some of whom had been at it for multiple decades—could give her their hard-won advice and perspective. And now that she's a veteran herself, she can turn around and give that gift to the newer caregivers in the group.

As Laura says, "To heal from my post-traumatic stress, I had to get outside myself. When I'm giving back to people, I lose focus on my own problems and instead lose myself in others. When I listen to their stories and what they're going through, I expand my capacity for compassion and empathy. When I was with other caregivers, I didn't feel so overcome by own problems. And little by little, over the course of about three years, I was...done. What I'd gone through just ceased to be that big of a deal to me."

And me, as you can probably already guess, I found community with other TBI survivors and in the new connections I made with my speaking path. I'm still a regular at a couple of TBI survivor groups, and I've clocked close to a thousand hours (and counting) as a volunteer at IMC. One of the groups I attend regularly meets at the same time and place as Laura's caregiver support group. The survivors and caregivers split off into their separate groups and do their own thing. Since the caregiver group meeting usually goes longer than the survivor group, we hang out in the waiting area for our people to be done. I like to say, "Isn't it incredible what our caretakers are doing in there? I make jokes, but it's serious at the same time. They're in there right now saving our marriages and partnerships, keeping us off the streets, keeping us from being homeless, turning to drugs, or going to prison." Every month, I say, "Let's let them meet for as long they need to."

* * *

Laura and I have done a good job of nurturing our relationship after TBI, but when you look at us from the outside, the picture is probably rosier and clearer than it is in real life. I realize that, in some ways, I appear to be the model TBI survivor. I'm perceived to be damn near the pinnacle of what's possible for recovery. And

Laura is the model caregiver. She's been a force for good not only for me but for other caregivers. But because of Laura's pushing folks away, and my putting on my best face in the workplace and in public, few people really knew the extent of the trauma and hardship we endured. So, there's a relatively shiny surface, but the reality is that there have been low moments. Very low moments.

To this day, we go through cycles, where Laura still gets frustrated with having to accommodate my needs as a TBI survivor, complicated by the fact that brain injury has become such a major feature of our life, especially with me cultivating a pathway around it. Tensions can flare. A mundane incident may take on greater importance in the context of our new life, where financial constraints are in place, where we don't have the same support network of friends, where our activities are more limited. Sometimes one or both of us can drop into a mode of seeing seemingly mundane events through a filter of grief, which highlights what we've lost. Sometimes I suspect that Laura is still hoping that some more of the "old" Greg will come back. She may still be struggling with true acceptance of the new Greg. She's had to fall in love with me twice. She had to get used to dealing with Greg #1's quirks, and now she's dealing with Greg #2. My nuero-psych recently pointed out, in some ways, I still need to accept the new me—my physical and cognitive abilities continue to slide at times. Go figure. But I have the right battling tools.

When I see Laura having a low moment, I know it's time for a role reversal—it's time for me to act as the caregiver. I try my best to soothe her even though I know I don't really have the power to change the circumstances that are so painful for her. But I owe it to her to try, and to be patient with her. She's done that much, and a hell of a lot more, for me.

* * *

One of the ways we make meaning out of a traumatic experience is by sharing our story with others. I chose to pursue a new direction as a speaker and author, and so I tell my story by choice. I volunteer and mentor by choice. But my story isn't possible without Laura. It isn't possible without a lot of people. The front cover of this book would be very crowded if it listed the name of every person who helped me tell this story. The stage at every speaking event would be very crowded if it held every person who helped me get there. But I most certainly can't spread a message of nurturing relationships after TBI without my partner by my side.

Of course, people want to hear the gory details of the accident. So, retelling the story has become part of the narrative of our lives. Laura has to retell the worst moments of her life in order to be able to use it as the foundation for making meaning of it. She doesn't want her entire life to revolve around my head injury; she's the kind of person who likes to let the past stay in the past. Unfortunately, that's not possible when the brain injury lives on, even in light of the fact that I've made incredible improvements and recovered extensively.

With my speaking pathway now embedded in our lives, she has to get on board with the fact that she will be called upon to ride along. She's in the sidecar and doesn't necessarily want to be. But my story can only be told in tandem; I can't do it alone. And so Laura walks a fine line—on one hand, she has to tend to herself and her drive to go forward and create the future; on the other, she knows that she and I have a valuable message to share, and that her voice simply can't be replaced. She has to constantly dance between stepping away from it so that it doesn't dominate her life, and stepping forward, into the limelight with me, in order to help other survivors and caregivers make meaning of their experience, find community, and heal while navigating life-altering injuries.

Whenever Laura and I give our presentation on relationships, people line up to talk. These are such intimate moments, with people at all parts of the brain injury journey. They tell us their stories, we cry together, we hug. During these conversations, I look over and watch Laura as she handles these moments with grace, empathy, and focused, loving attention. She is a true caregiver—holding a hand, touching a shoulder, letting someone process in whatever way works for them, whether that's with tears, humor, or both.

Tens of thousands of people sustain brain injuries every day, and so there are always people starting out on their own TBI journeys. Once, at an event, a woman and her two teenage boys came up to Laura and me and said, "We're new to this." It's a good reminder that there are always new chances to take what we've learned and turn around to give a hand to those who are coming up behind us.

Brain injury is a great equalizer. It affects so many different people, of all ages and walks of life. Doesn't matter your social or economic class, your race, your belief system, your political persuasion. None of these distinctions make a bit of difference. And it can happen to any one of us at any time. It simply does not discriminate.

While none of us would wish for a traumatic brain injury, it is one of life's many avenues for opportunity, should we choose to see it that way. There are new peaks to summit, new moments to cherish and celebrate, and—best of all—new chances to open up and connect with people. I thought I was living a successful life before TBI, but now I see that when you lose everything you thought you had, what's left are the people who love you.

About the Authors

Greg Nordfelt

Greg is a Professional Member of the National Speakers Association and is on the Board of Directors of the National Speakers Association Mountain West Chapter. Greg has 37 years of public speaking experience through his Senior Management career with Zions Bank and NSA.

Greg knows firsthand the importance of motivation and teamwork in achieving huge goals. In 2011, a motorcycle accident left Greg with his 3rd traumatic brain injury. When he rejoined the world after 11 days in and out of a coma. Greg found himself radically changed. Greg's story isn't one of loss and pain. Instead, it's a symbol of incredible gain. He had a newfound focus on love, connection and gratitude. He relearned how to speak, read, write and walk again and returned to his senior banking position, which is extremely rare. He has authored two books. He has been on several TV News and Magazine reports and various publications. Greg received his Finance and MBA degrees from the University of Utah. He was awarded Survivor of the Year by the Brain Injury Alliance of Utah and was Utah Speech Pathology and Audiology USHA's Ambassador.

His clients include The Governor's Office of Economic Development, healthcare organizations, S&P 500 companies, Major Universities, National Speakers Association Speaker's Showcase, Chambers of Commerce and many more.

Sheila Ashdown

Sheila is a Portland, Oregon–based writer and editor. She has co-authored four books and edited dozens more. She holds an MFA in creative writing from American University and is currently at work on a novel.

ADDITIONAL RESOURCES

Would you benefit from a quick and easy guide to empower you in your recovery or make life easier as a TBI care-giver? Well, here it is!

I've designed a FREE guide with you in mind,

7 Keys to Overcoming TBI & Life's Challenges.

Go to gregnordfelt.com/7keys to get your free copy.

Here's to having a great life, no matter what it brings.

Ride on!

Greg Nordfelt

Made in the USA
Coppell, TX
13 December 2021

68361243R00090